—The Civil War Story of—
BLOODY BILL ANDERSON

Larry Wood

Eakin Press ⬥ Fort Worth, Texas
www.EakinPress.com

Copyright © 2003
By Larry Wood
Published By Eakin Press
An Imprint of Wild Horse Media Group
P.O. Box 331779
Fort Worth, Texas 76163
1-817-344-7036
www.EakinPress.com
ALL RIGHTS RESERVED
1 2 3 4 5 6 7 8 9
ISBN-10: 1571686401
ISBN-13: 978-1571686404

Library of Congress Cataloging-in-Publication Data
Wood, Larry.
  The Civil War story of Bloody Bill Anderson / Larry Wood.–1st ed.
    p. cm.
  Includes bibliographical references and index.
    ISBN 1-57168-640-1
    1. Anderson, William T. 2. Guerrillas–Confederate States of America–Biography. 3. Soldiers–Confederate States of America–Biography.
4. Confederate States of America. Army–Biography. 5. United States–History–Civil War, 1861-1865–Underground movements. 6. West (U.S.)–History–Civil War, 1861-1865–Underground movements.
7. Quantrill, William Clarke, 1837-1865–Friends and associates. I. Title
E470.45.A53 W66 2002
973.7'37'092–dc21   2002014063

To G. G. for believing in me.

Contents

Preface vii
Acknowledgments ix
Introduction xi
Chapter One: My Native State of Missouri 1
Chapter Two: They Murdered My Father 7
Chapter Three: The Last Man You Ever Will See 17
Chapter Four: The Most Desperate of Desperate Men 21
Chapter Five: They Murdered My Sister 29
Chapter Six: I Have Glutted My Vengeance 38
Chapter Seven: Quantrill's Sand Is Gone 49
Chapter Eight: I Had Them to Kill 64
Chapter Nine: Things I Would Shrink from
    If Possible to Avoid 79
Chapter Ten: I Will Hunt You Down Like Wolves 92
Chapter Eleven: Every Federal Soldier Shall
    Die Like a Dog 106

Chapter Twelve: I Grew Sick of Killing Them 117
Chapter Thirteen: I Could Not Throw My Life Away 123
Chapter Fourteen: One Devil Less in the World 136

Notes 143
Bibliography 159
Index 163
About the Author 171

Preface

One might reasonably ask, Why another book about Bloody Bill Anderson, who was, after all, a minor figure in the big picture of America's Civil War?

The answer to the question lies partly in the simple fact that I began research for this book a number of years ago when no complete biography of Anderson existed, and, after publication of Castel and Goodrich's biography in 1998, I decided, nevertheless, to continue the project. I do not in any way suggest that my book is better or more complete than the previous work. I do know that this book contains quite a bit of information about Anderson and his family that is not included in the earlier work, just as the Castel and Goodrich book contains information that is not included in mine. Also, I think the reader will find that my book offers a somewhat different perspective that, while certainly not condoning or excusing the heinous deeds of Anderson, portrays him perhaps in a slightly more sympathetic light.

In answer to the larger question of why anyone would want to write about Bill Anderson in the first place, let me say that I am not as fascinated with the big picture of the Civil War as I am with its effect on individual lives. I am interested not so much in weaponry, troop movements, and military strategy as I am in human emotion and the disintegrating effects of the war on the moral and social fabric of the American people. The Civil War sometimes brought out the best in people, but more often, the worst. It laid bare their old hatreds, gave rise to new ones, and bred inhuman violence. Nowhere was this truer than in the border state of Missouri, where arose a vicious brand of guerrilla warfare that was fueled by revenge and marked by atrocity, and the Civil War offers no starker example of its dehumanizing influence than in the story of Missouri's leading purveyor of bloodshed, William T. Anderson.

Acknowledgments

To thank all the people who contributed in some small way to this work would be next to impossible, but I'd like express my appreciation in particular to the staffs of the Kansas State Historical Society, the State Historical Society of Missouri, the reference section of the Joplin Public Library, and the local and family history room of the same facility for their unfailing cooperation during my research efforts.

Introduction

The state of Missouri was secured for the Union during the early days of America's Civil War. Southern sympathies remained widespread, though, among citizens of the border state, and a particularly vicious brand of guerrilla warfare arose in response to the Federal occupation.

The largest and most notorious band of Missouri guerrillas was led by an enigmatic ex-schoolteacher from Kansas named William Quantrill. The gang carried out raids, such as the infamous sacking of Lawrence, against Union targets along the Missouri-Kansas border and provided a training ground for post-war desperadoes like the Youngers and the James brothers.

After Lawrence, though, Quantrill's standing among the guerrillas slipped, and one of his lieutenants, William "Bloody Bill" Anderson, rose to power. Throwing off his leader's authority to establish his own band, Anderson went on to surpass even the notorious Quantrill in heinous deeds, culminating in the Centralia massacre during September of 1864. Anderson, whom Cole Younger called "the most desperate of desperate men," was killed a month later when leading a wild charge against a company of Federal cavalry.

The story of the Missouri guerrillas continues to fascinate

students of the Civil War and the Old West alike, and Quantrill and his men have been the subject of numerous books. Bill Anderson always warrants special mention in the Quantrill biographies, but his story has only recently begun to be told in its own right.

Anderson is often depicted in the Quantrill books as a hardened criminal, even before the war, who became a homicidal maniac during it. There's some truth to this portrayal, but it is a simplification. A fascinating story of human tragedy and unbridled revenge lies beneath the caricature of madness.

CHAPTER ONE

My Native State of Missouri

When Bill Anderson was a boy in the late 1840s and early 1850s, his grammar school classmates in Missouri considered him more reserved and better behaved than average. In the late 1850s, according to a neighbor in Kansas, he was a steady, hardworking young man. But by the time he died just a few years later near the end of America's Civil War, people far and wide called him an inhuman monster, and one observer deemed him the worst criminal in the history of mankind. What happened?

William "Bill" Anderson was born in 1839 to William C. and Martha Anderson, in Hopkins County, Kentucky, where his parents had married on December 1, 1836. When Bill was just a newborn, the family moved to Palmyra, Missouri, along with his maternal grandparents, William and Mahala Thomasson. There Thomasson went into business as a hatter, and Bill's father, who later listed his occupation as a hatter, too, presumably helped out in the enterprise.[1]

The venture didn't last long, though, and the Andersons soon moved on to Iowa Territory, where Bill's brothers, Ellis and James, were born. By the mid-1840s, the family was back in Missouri, settling this time in Randolph County, where Bill's sisters Mary Ellen, Josephine, and Martha Jane were born.[2]

Ancestors of William T. Anderson

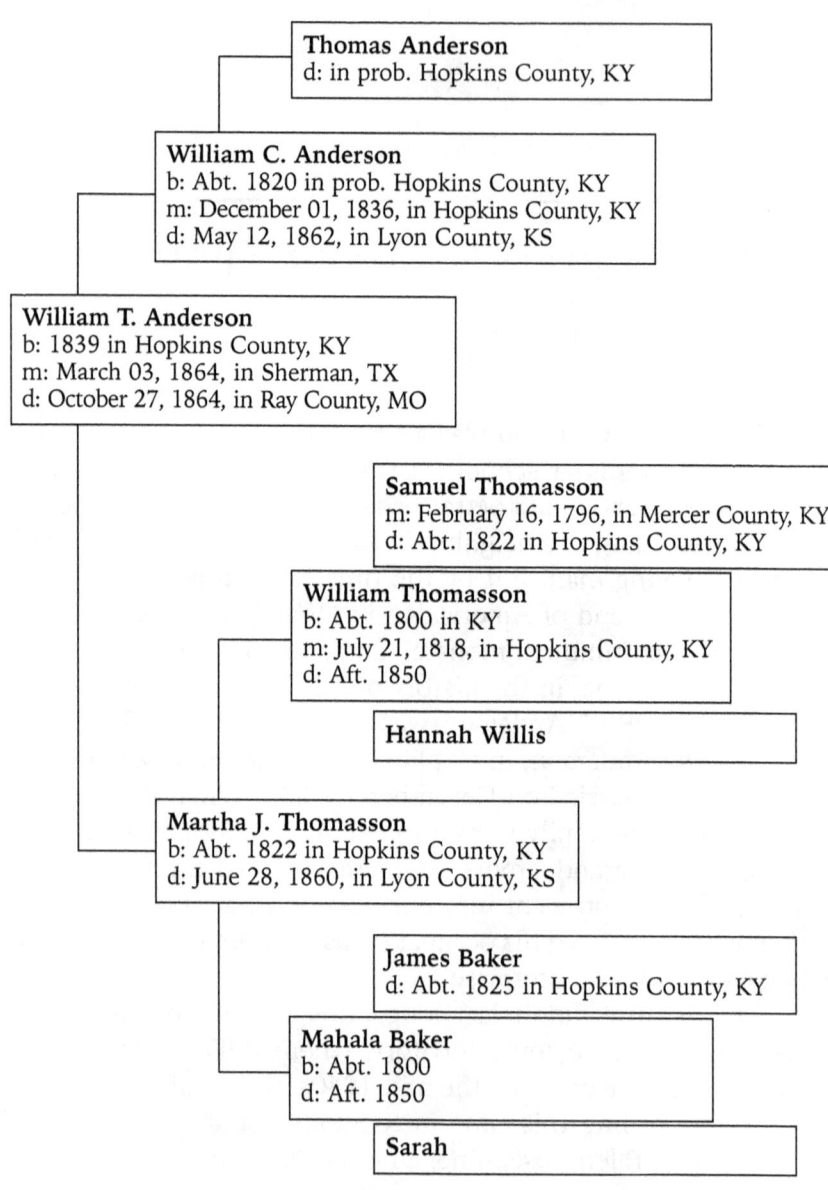

In 1847 William C. Anderson was a charter member of Randolph Lodge 23 of the Independent Order of Odd Fellows. Although both he and his father-in-law still listed their occupation as hatter, Anderson spent most of his time scratching out a living on a rented farm.

About 1850 the elder Anderson traipsed off to the gold mines of California with Henry Austin and several other local men, in search of quick riches. Bill's restless father came back with a taste for the frontier but without much gold.

The community around Huntsville, though, thought well of the family. Austin's son Tad was a schoolmate of Bill Anderson and considered him a pal. Years later, Tad Austin's only remarkable recollection of the young Anderson was that Bill "seemed to be more quiet and better behaved than the general run."[3]

In 1856 William C. Anderson, struck with another case of wanderlust, journeyed west again, leaving Bill as the head of the family. He went off to New Mexico with freighter Charlie Parker, then on the way back stopped and built a cabin deep in Kansas Territory. He returned in the fall with plans to move the family out there in search of a new dream. Fertile land was opening up to the west, just there for the taking for anybody willing to move out and claim it.

In the early spring of 1857, the Andersons loaded up their belongings and headed southwest.[4] The fight over "Bleeding Kansas" yet raged even as the Anderson wagon rolled down the Santa Fe Trail into Kansas.

In 1821 the Missouri Compromise had stipulated that Missouri be admitted to the Union as a slave state but that no new slave states be admitted north of Missouri's southern boundary. But later, in 1854, Congress had passed the Kansas-Nebraska Act, opening up Missouri's neighboring territory for white settlement and establishing the principle of "popular sovereignty." The people of the territory would decide for themselves whether to allow slavery within its borders. So, for the past three years, the country's debate over slavery had been played out in Kansas.

Northerners had been outraged that the Kansas-Nebraska

Act repealed conditions of the Missouri Compromise, which they considered a binding agreement. They swarmed into the new territory by the wagonload, vowing to make Kansas free soil.

At the same time, people in western Missouri like the Andersons felt a natural bond with their neighboring territory. The eastern one-third of Kansas was similar in terrain and climate to western Missouri. The few white people who already lived in the area at the time it was officially opened up for settlement had mostly drifted across the border from Missouri. Geography, culture, and sometimes family ties united the two regions.

Many Missourians resented the influx of "outsiders" to Kansas, and they flooded across the border in response. The race was on to see which side would control territorial politics. Wealthy landowners in the western part of Missouri, who saw in the prospect of a free Kansas a haven for runaway slaves, found the inflow of Northerners particularly disturbing, and they sustained and encouraged the migration of Missouri's yeoman farmers to the neighboring territory.

Like most early Missouri settlers, William C. Anderson and his wife had come from the upper tier of Southern states, and the family undoubtedly identified with the Southern culture and accepted the lower status of blacks as a given. Yet the Andersons, again like the vast majority of Missourians, were not slaveholders, and the question of slavery was probably not an overriding issue for the family.[5] It was not so much politics that made the Andersons pick up stakes and move in 1857 as the lure of the frontier and the prospect of cheap land.

Yet, even homesteaders like the Andersons could not help but be aware of the conflict in Kansas. Leavenworth and Atchison, pro-slavery strongholds during the early struggle for control of the territory, lay to the north as the family struck the Santa Fe Trail. Farther west, the Andersons passed the rival town of Lawrence, which border ruffians had plundered on May 21, 1856, because of the town's predominant abolitionist sentiment. To the south lay Pottawatomie Creek, where three days after the Lawrence raid, John Brown had sought revenge by hacking five pro-slavery settlers to death with a sword and cutting off their fingers. Still farther along the road, the Anderson party passed Topeka, another bastion of Northern settlers.

Political strife over Kansas statehood persisted even in 1857. Bands of vigilantes representing either side of the slavery issue patrolled roads and rivers, stopping newcomers to interrogate them and to try to intimidate the new arrivals into turning back if the wrong answer were given. Settlers already established in the territory were subject to arson, theft, and other crimes as each side tried to run off the other.

But the Andersons passed through unmolested and arrived finally in the Council Grove area at the very edge of the frontier, more than two hundred miles from the home they had left in northern Missouri. Not many settlers had yet made it this far west. The previous summer, the elder Anderson had built an isolated cabin in the southwestern quadrant of the intersection of Bluff Creek and the Santa Fe Trail. From the banks of the creek, a north fork of the Neosho River, he could see miles and miles of gently rolling plains, a blue sky that seemed to go on forever, and not another human being except his own family.

The few people already in the area, though, were mostly from the Northern states, and the Andersons' state of origin quickly put them at odds with some of their neighbors. Throughout the struggle for Kansas, Northern settlers considered the frontiersmen who streamed across the border from Missouri poor white trash whose favorite pastimes were fighting and drinking whiskey—dirty, lazy miscreants, given to coarse language and gross behavior. The conviction around Bluff Creek was no exception to the common opinion. Northerners like L. D. Bailey thought the Andersons to be "of a rough type."[6]

In this conception of things, the Northern settlers saw themselves as morally and intellectually superior to "pukes" like the Andersons. The New Englanders were industrious people, full of Yankee ingenuity and enterprise. Fighters against the barbarous institution of slavery, they were Puritan heroes who had right on their side.

To Missouri settlers, though, the Northerners were hypocritical do-gooders who used their sanctimonious opposition to slavery to justify the theft of property and the "liberation" of blacks. The abolitionists' concern for the Negro, they believed, disguised an unholy lust for black women.

In this interpretation, Missourians like the Andersons saw themselves as the upholders of law and order and defenders of the family. It was they who were protecting traditional values from the invading Yankee radicals. Such preconceived notions aggravated the animosity Northerners and Missourians felt for each other in Kansas, but by 1858, open struggle between the two sides had waned. The unorganized pro-slavery forces could not match the continual inflow of free-soilers from the Northern states, and the Free-State Party gained the upper hand in territorial politics. Many pro-slavery settlers were driven from the region.

But the Andersons stayed on, and gradually they learned that not all their neighbors were Yankee radicals. Even A. I. Baker, who served Breckinridge County as probate judge in the name of the Free-State Party, nursed Southern leanings. A Virginia native and former slaveholder, Baker lived five miles west of the Andersons on Rock Creek. He had named the location Agnes City after his mother, and he ran a roadside store on the site, catering to passing wagons on the Santa Fe Trail. The Andersons became friends with Baker, and William C. Anderson served on the first grand jury in the county in 1858.[7]

Eli Sewell, Baker's brother-in-law, hired Bill Anderson to stay on a ranch Sewell owned west of Council Grove and to run the place for him. Sewell, born in Ohio, considered Bill "a steady boy, steady as a clock."[8]

Life for the Andersons took on a satisfying routine, and the territory settled into a tentative peace. Then in January of 1861, Kansas entered the Union as a free state.

Many folks living along the Missouri-Kansas border, though, were just waiting for an excuse to revisit "Bleeding Kansas." They still held grudges and itched to settle old scores from a conflict that stretched back seven years. The echo of South Carolina cannons just three months after Kansas statehood gave them their excuse.

CHAPTER TWO

They Murdered My Father

The capture of Fort Sumter set off celebrations in western Missouri and fanned the flames of secessionist sentiment. Demonstrations of support for the Southern cause broke out, and hundreds of young men rushed to join Gen. Sterling Price's state militia, which had aligned with the Rebel army. Federal troops from surrounding states, though, drove Price to the southwestern part of Missouri, securing the northern part for the Union. Pro-Southern boys and men left behind in the Jackson County area formed into bands of guerrillas to harass the invading Federal forces.

Meanwhile, Kansans saw in the outbreak of war a chance to punish western Missouri for its past misdeeds and current secessionist zeal. With many of the area's fighting men gone south with Price, the border counties were left vulnerable, and Kansas troops raided throughout the region in the summer and fall of 1861.

In June, Charles "Doc" Jennison and his infamous jayhawkers, known officially as the Seventh Kansas Cavalry, burned homes, plundered stores, and terrorized citizens around Kansas City and areas to the south. Later, a company of scouts known as "Red Legs," because of the red leather leggings they wore,

Looking toward Bluff Creek along the old Santa Fe Trail as it appears today. This is the approximate spot where the Andersons lived in Kansas.

perpetrated atrocities along the border area under Jennison disciple Lt. George Hoyt.

Kansas' newly elected U.S. senator Jim Lane recruited the Kansas Brigade and sacked and burned the town of Osceola in southwestern Missouri in September. John Brown Jr., son of the fanatic abolitionist, and James Montgomery, a disciple of the elder Brown, carried out similar raids. Daniel Anthony, brother of Susan B. Anthony, and ex-convict Marshall Cleveland also had bands that committed depredations throughout western Missouri on Union and Southern citizens alike.

By November of 1861, the region had been laid waste. A young lady writing to her mother from Westport, south of Kansas City complained, "We have been overrun with jayhawkers."[1] The forays into Missouri had become for the Kansas troops little more than a lark.

By Christmas, though, a cloud of retribution already hovered over the Sni Hills of eastern Jackson County, in the form of a mysterious man named William Quantrill. Returning from Price's army, he formed a band of guerrillas during the winter and began to vex Federal forces in the area by stopping mail wagons, cutting telegraph wires, destroying bridges, and otherwise harrying Union targets.

The indiscriminate pillaging of the Kansas troops during the previous fall and summer had driven even conditional Unionists into the Southern camp, and young men from the Jackson County area flocked to the rising guerrilla leader with tales of Union ill-treatment. Quantrill soon gathered about him some of the deadliest young men along the border—men like Cole Younger and George Todd.

An ex-schoolteacher from Kansas who had run afoul of the law around Lawrence prior to the war, Quantrill harbored a singular resentment toward the state. On an early morning in March of 1862, with a force of about forty men, he dashed across the border to the small hamlet of Aubrey, ransacked the village, shot his former school superintendent in the head, and took a Union officer for ransom. Not only had Quantrill within a few short weeks become the number-one enemy of Federal authorities in

Jackson County, he had now taken the war back to Kansas, where many Missourians along the border felt it had begun.

*****

Back at Council Grove, on the edge of the frontier, the sounds of fighting were scarcely a rumble. Yet, portentous events had disturbed the Andersons' tranquil life even before civil war rent the country apart.

While working on Sewell's ranch west of Council Grove, Bill Anderson had a run-in with Kaw Indians, who were prevalent in the area. Anderson had gone to Council Grove for a jug of molasses and was on his way back to the ranch when two Indians, one on foot and one riding a pony, approached and, believing the jug contained liquor, tried to take it from him. One of them held the bit of Anderson's horse while the other tried to cut the jug from the saddle. Anderson spurred his horse and broke away, but the Indians gave chase, with the one on foot gaining ground. Anderson turned in the saddle and fired a gun over his shoulder, meaning, he claimed, just to scare his fleet pursuer. But the man on foot dropped dead, while his companion scampered away on horseback. The die was cast.

At about the same time, Ellis Anderson was involved in a similar incident. Bill was away from Sewell's ranch, and his brother was staying there during Bill's absence. One day Ellis had been out in the fields and walked into the cabin to find an Indian drinking whiskey from a bottle that belonged to Anderson. Ellis Anderson drove the intruder out, but the man came back drunk after dark and kept trying to get into the cabin. Finally young Anderson stuck a gun through a crack in the wall and shot the bothersome Indian. Afterward, Anderson fled the territory and was reportedly killed in a row of some sort near Council Bluffs, Iowa.[2]

From the fall of 1859 to the fall of 1860, a prolonged drought on the plains made farming difficult and drove many settlers back east. In order to make ends meet, William C. Anderson, who had never really taken to farming anyway, depended more and more on a wayside business he had set up. He sold whiskey and other provisions out of a small store and kept a hand in Charlie Parker's freighting operation.[3]

Anderson never went on the wagon trains himself, but his son did. On one trip into New Mexico about 1860, Bill Anderson was made second boss and a man named Dick Pratt, first boss. South of Santa Fe they "lost" the wagon train, so they said, claiming that the mules and horses had strayed, and they came back home on foot.

Upon his return Anderson became, in the words of Eli Sewell, "a desperate fellow." Horses were in high demand on the frontier, and Bill seized the opportunity. He quit regular work and went into horse trading. With the help of his younger brother Jim, he would gather a few ponies, take them to Missouri, and come back with good horses to sell around Council Grove.[4]

Bill's brother Ellis had died or disappeared by 1860, and during the summer of that year, tragedy struck the Anderson family a second time. On June 28 Mrs. Anderson was out in the yard, gathering chips with which to start a fire, when she was hit by lightning and killed instantly. The July 2 issue of the *Kansas Press* reported the incident under the headline "Death by Lightning":

> A sad affair occurred on Thursday of last week, resulting in the instant death of a Mrs. Anderson near the crossing of the Santa Fe road at Bluff Creek—Mrs. Anderson was but a few yards from the house, thoughtless of danger. The current struck her upon the side of the head, passing downwards, completely scathing that side, and passing through the foot in two places.

The July 7 issue of the *Emporia News* added additional details in its account of the accident: "The lightning struck her on the head, burning the hair from a place large as a man's hand, and passing downward tore her breast and hip frightfully."

Mischance seemed to shadow the Anderson family like a curse. A young man named George DeMoyne, a member of the

Anderson gang, came into Council Grove to get a shroud for the mother's burial. He was quickly arrested and strung up to a tree in a mock lynching to try to get him to tell about the suspected horse-snatching activities of the Andersons, but he wouldn't talk. Finally, he was let down.

With the war coming on, the Andersons stepped up their horse dealing, running animals to the west as well as to Missouri, and more and more, their horse "trading" took on the aspect of horse stealing. The boys would round up or steal ponies, take them west of Council Grove, and sell them to accomplices along the Santa Fe Trail, who then took them on toward New Mexico for resale. Lee Griffin, a cousin of Bill and Jim Anderson who had once lived with A. I. Baker but who was now staying with the Anderson family, was in on the scheme.[5]

The shenanigans of the Anderson brothers, however, did not immediately destroy the family's good name. Judge Baker, who earlier in the year had bought the *Council Grove Press* and taken up residence in the town, had kind words for his neighbors in an article he wrote in the June 22, 1861, edition of the paper, describing his recent trip to Lawrence:

> After leaving the Grove the first place we drew up at was Agnes City, the gem of Breckinridge, our home and heart is here. Bluff Creek, five miles east of Agnes, is also beautiful. We spent two or three hours at this place rambling over the well cultivated fields and garden of our esteemed friend William C. Anderson, whose pleasant family know how to entertain their friends.

Baker may have had a hidden motive for extolling the Andersons. His wife had recently died, and he had developed more than a passing interest in sixteen-year-old Mary "Molly" Anderson. Before long, the thirty-seven-year-old Baker had seduced the pretty young girl and was again enjoying intimate relations, this time without benefit of matrimony. One report claims that Mary Anderson even left home and moved in with Baker with the expectation, if not the promise, of marriage. The judge himself was rumored to be involved in the Andersons' horse-running operation.

During the early days of the war, Bill Anderson spoke often of joining the Confederate guerrillas, but for no heartfelt or noble reason. He tried to talk acquaintance C. H. Strieby, a Council Grove blacksmith, into joining with him. "I don't care anymore than you do for the South, Strieby," Anderson said, "but there's a lot of money in this business."[6]

Strieby refused, but others were more easily persuaded to the idea of Confederate service. Bill Anderson, Griffin, Baker, and a secessionist friend of Baker named John W. Ratliff, in answer to General Price's urgent call for volunteers, rode south in the late fall of 1861 to join Gen. James S. Rains of the Missouri State Guard, from whom Baker had supposedly obtained a commission as a major.[7] After spending the night in Jasper County, Missouri, at the farm of Josiah Pinson, they started with Pinson's son Richard, a Southern soldier home on leave, toward Osceola to join the State Guard camp there.[8] They got as far as Vernon County and were camped at Dry Wood Creek, not far from the Kansas state line.

They were attacked there by a company of the Sixth Kansas Cavalry under Capt. L. R. Jewell. Ratliff was shot and killed and Baker captured. The rest of the party got away and accompanied Pinson to his unit at Osceola. Anderson and Griffin spent a few days with Price's army and then hightailed it back to the Council Grove area.

Baker spent four months as a prisoner at Fort Scott before the influence of friends helped get him released. Around the first of April, 1862, the chastened judge returned, took up residence once again at Rock Creek, and undertook to earn his way back into the good graces of the Union folk around Breckinridge County, who in February had changed the name of their county to Lyon in honor of Union general Nathaniel Lyon, killed the previous summer at Wilson's Creek in southwestern Missouri.[9]

Baker commenced his reparation by throwing off the "bitter rebel" Molly Anderson in favor of Annis Segur, a seventeen-year-old schoolteacher and daughter of Ira Segur, a farmer from

New York.[10] The judge also wrote a letter to the *Emporia News*, reasserting his support of the Union and seeking to explain his motive for going to Missouri, but as a story in the paper had reported at the time of Baker's capture, "a suit of secession soldier clothes which he had on, and other suspicious circumstances, are against him."[11]

The judge was clearly trying to distance himself from his old comrades, though, and it didn't take long for the Anderson gang to answer Baker's betrayal. On May 7, 1862, Segur reported a span of horses stolen, and Lee Griffin was the suspected culprit. Search parties went out to comb the area, looking for the thief. One of the missing horses had a distinctive hoof print, and Segur and Eli Sewell picked up the trail of the two horses west of Council Grove. They sent word back to Baker at town, who came out with another man to follow the trail.

Beyond the Cottonwood River near Delaware Holes, Baker met one of the horses coming back toward home with a Mexican man trailing after it. The judge and his companion captured the Mexican and tied him up at a nearby small ranch. Leaving the captive there, they went on west and met Lee Griffin. Baker tried to interrogate the young man, but he refused to speak at first and denied his identify when he finally did talk.

Continuing west without detaining Griffin, Baker and his companion found the second horse in a wagon train camp near the Little Arkansas River, more than eighty miles from Council Grove. The traders in the caravan said they had bought the horse that very day from a stranger, and they gave a description that fit Lee Griffin.

When Baker got back home, he jailed the Mexican in an upstairs room of his house under the guard of a constable. Then he swore out a warrant for the arrest of Griffin.

In the meantime, Griffin had made it back to Council Grove well ahead of the Baker party and had sought the protection of his cousins Bill and Jim Anderson. The Anderson brothers sprang to the aid of their cohort, hiding him out in ravines and among the timber of creeks. Search parties spotted the fugitives on several occasions, but the superior mounts of the Andersons outran their pursuers. Bill Anderson's horse was a large chestnut, with two white hind feet, that Anderson often entered in races. Called Silver Heels, it was, according to neighbor O. F. O'Dell, "the fastest horse . . . in the Western States."[12]

Early Sunday morning May 11, an armed search party went to the Anderson home and informed William C. Anderson of the warrant for Griffin's arrest, told him that his sons were aiding and abetting a horse thief, and implicated the sons in the theft. Anderson resented the men's accusations, and he cursed and shoved aside their rifles. Still fuming that A. I. Baker had taken advantage of his oldest daughter and then jilted her for a Yankee schoolteacher, he demanded to know who had issued the warrant for Griffin. The answer threw him into a rage.

That night, the irate Anderson went to Rock Creek full of whiskey, with a loaded double-barrel shotgun. His sons Bill and Jim, who had come in from the bushes, accompanied him, but Lee Griffin was still hiding out. The elder Anderson confronted Baker and told the judge that if he didn't take back the warrant on Griffin, he would kill him. Baker wouldn't back down, but Bill Anderson interceded and prevented his father from carrying out the threat.

The next day shortly before noon, though, while Bill was busy trying to get Griffin out of the area, the elder Anderson went back to Agnes City with his cocked and loaded shotgun, swearing again to kill A. I. Baker, who was in an upstairs room. In reporting the incident at the time, the *Emporia News* said that Anderson sought Baker's life for branding the father and his sons as horse thieves "and perhaps one or two other reasons which it is not necessary to make public."[13]

When Anderson started up the stairs, the constable in charge of the Mexican grabbed the intruder and held him around the waist to prevent him from going up. Suddenly Baker appeared at the head of the stairs with a gun of his own, and the constable stepped aside, out of harm's way. Baker got the drop on Anderson and shot him through the heart, killing him instantly.[14]

Later that day, Bill Anderson came in for the burial of his father at 142 Mile Creek, east of his home, and was served there with a warrant for his arrest for aiding and abetting horse theft. The warrant, however, was found defective, and Anderson was released until it could be redrawn.

Afterward, C. H. Withington, a New York native and one of the first settlers of Breckinridge County, complained about legal technicalities that would allow a horse thief to go free. Withington, who ran a store in the area, had played some role in the issuance of the warrant in the first place, and he suggested that there had been a time in Kansas when Anderson would have been strung up on the spot. Anderson attacked the old man with a broom handle for offering such an unpalatable opinion, then mounted up and rode toward Agnes City.

There he delivered himself to authorities, seeking protection from the angry mob he claimed was being raised on 142 Mile Creek to hang him, and, according to Sewell, he "made up" with Baker over his father's death, which had occured earlier that day. That some sort of tentative reconciliation occurred is evidenced by the fact that Anderson retained Baker's old law partner, Robert M. Ruggles, for his defense and was released on bail.

By nightfall, the mob Anderson feared had indeed collected, but not at 142 Mile creek. About thirty men, swearing vengeance against all horse thieves, showed up at Agnes City. Shortly after dark, they wrested the Mexican from the custody of the constable, dragged him to some woods, and strung him up to the nearest tree.

Learning of the lynching, Bill Anderson lay low in fear that authorities might not be able to protect him from a similar fate. While in hiding, he began to ruminate on all that Baker had done against his family, and the chew left a bitter taste. A couple of days later, he showed back up at Baker's for the inquest into his father's death, which occurred about the same time as the wedding of Baker and Annis Segur.[15] When the jury announced that Baker had acted in self-defense, Anderson and his brother swore revenge, but the judge said he didn't seriously think the boys would hurt him.

A. I. Baker was the last man to underestimate Bill Anderson's capacity for violence.

CHAPTER THREE

The Last Man You Ever Will See

After the verdict absolving Baker of guilt, Anderson decided that he and his brother were no longer safe around the Bluff Creek area. Making arrangements for his sisters to follow, he and Jim mounted their fleet horses and fled for the Missouri border. After ensconcing the rest of the family at the home of friends or relatives on the Kansas side of the line, the brothers took to the bush southwest of Kansas City, preying on Southern and loyal citizens alike.

Rumors of their marauding soon reached Quantrill and brought the Andersons face to face with the guerrilla leader. William Gregg, a lieutenant under Quantrill, recalled the encounter: "The first time I saw Bill Anderson was near Aubrey, Kansas in June or July, 1862. Quantrill dismounted him and his brother Jim, another man, and told them if he ever heard of them robbing anyone again he'd kill them."[1]

If Quantrill "dismounted" the threesome, either they quickly procured new horses, or the meeting described by Gregg occurred in July rather than June, because at the end of June, Anderson was on the trail riding back toward Council Grove with vengeance in his heart. On July 2, less than two months after he had fled the area, he returned with his brother Jim, Lee Griffin, a man named William Reed, and one other man.²

The Anderson gang arrived at Rock Creek on the Santa Fe Trail that evening but found Baker away from home. The five men lurked in the area, awaiting the judge's return from Emporia, and again called at the Baker residence the following night, July 3, around eight or nine o'clock.³ Anderson sent a man unknown to Baker to the door, posing as a member of a wagon train in need of whiskey and provisions. Baker got his pistol and, accompanied by his sixteen-year-old brother-in-law, George Segur, led the stranger from the house to the roadside store.

Baker sent the boy into the cellar to get whiskey, then started to follow. Suddenly the other four members of the gang stepped from the shadows. "I wasn't expecting to see you, Bill," the startled Baker is reported to have said.⁴

"But you do see me, Inghram Baker," Anderson snapped, "and I'm the last man you ever will see, goddamn your soul."

The gang opened fire. Two of the shots wounded Baker, but he managed to pull his revolver and return fire, hitting Jim Anderson in the thigh but not seriously wounding him. Baker staggered into the cellar as his brother-in-law stepped out to see what the commotion was. The boy was shot, too, and driven back into the cellar.

Anderson and his gang slammed shut the cellar door and piled barrels and heavy boxes on top of it before setting the store ablaze. The boy escaped through a small window at the rear of the cellar but died the next day from his wounds. Baker burned to death or may have killed himself to escape such a fate. His brother-in-law reported hearing a single shot from the cellar after he crawled through the window.

After making sure the store and cellar were aflame, the Anderson gang burned Baker's carriage and fired his large stone dwelling, his barn, and several other outhouses. Then they stole two horses and started back toward Missouri on the Santa Fe Trail, robbing and terrorizing people along the way.

They came first to a settler named Henry, from whom they stole clothing and money.

At Allen on 142 Mile Creek (so named by early traders because it was 142 miles from the Missouri River), they went to the store and saloon of O. F. O'Dell, where several men, including C. H. Withington, were playing cards, telling stories, drinking beer, and anticipating the gala Fourth of July celebration the following day at Council Grove. The gang held all the men on the premises at gunpoint while they ransacked the place and stole tobacco, whiskey, and other provisions.

One of the gang knocked the proprietor down with a pistol, and Jim Anderson threatened to kill Withington for his part in the issuance of the warrant for Bill Anderson's arrest. Again Bill was cast in the unlikely role of peacemaker as he interceded to prevent the murder. His younger brother had to satisfy himself by stealing Withington's rifle and helping to herd the captives into a small stable, where they were placed under guard.

The gang tried to set fire to O'Dell's house, but the green logs wouldn't fire. They got a straw tick ablaze, but a feather bed they tossed on top of it smothered the flame. The gang stole three horses belonging to the Kansas City and Santa Fe Mail Company, in place of which they left some of the tired mounts they had been riding. Shortly before daylight, they set the captives free, bade them a polite good night, and rode east at full speed.

At Elm Creek the desperadoes shot into the home of William Jacoby, who also had played some role in the warrant for Anderson's arrest. A Santa Fe wagon train camped nearby was credited with discouraging further assault and thus saving the man's life.

The fugitives exchanged horses again on Chicken Creek at the stage station of Benjamin O'Dell, father of O. F. O'Dell, and boasted openly of the murder of Baker.

At Dragoon Creek, just west of Burlingame, the gang traded horses again, leaving two of theirs in exchange for two belonging to the Kansas City and Council Grove Stage Company.

Then they skirted Burlingame and threatened a bystander that they would destroy the town if the property of a man named Rice, who was accused of complicity with the Andersons, was disturbed.

The July 12, 1862, *Emporia News* concludes the narrative: "At 110 creek they compelled Mr. Harris to get breakfast for them in double-quick time—threatening to blow his brains out if he did not do so. They left there a little after daylight, and were probably in Missouri by noon of that day."

CHAPTER FOUR

The Most Desperate of Desperate Men

After escaping from Kansas, the Anderson gang, perhaps to avoid a territorial dispute and another confrontation with Quantrill, drifted east of Jackson County to resume the life of murder and plunder they had begun at Council Grove. In September of 1862, Anderson and his small gang captured four soldiers of Col. Henry Neill's Enrolled Missouri Militia southwest of Lexington in Lafayette County. The guerrillas took the militiamen to the Mayview vicinity and shot them, and the bodies were not discovered until a month later.[1] By the following winter, Anderson's band had killed a total of at least seven Union men and robbed loyal citizens throughout the Lafayette County area.

Around the first of the year of 1863, Lee Griffin was killed in a minor fray, but the editor of the *Lexington Weekly Union* was little cheered by the news. Describing the Anderson gang as "a different one from Quantrill's," the editor claimed, "there is no act of arson, robery [sic] or murder, from which they shrink."[2] He identified the small band as mainly from Kansas and named Reed, the Anderson brothers, and two other men as members of the gang.

It is unclear what happened to Reed, the purported leader of the gang's operations in Lafayette County, and it is also unclear whether the gang was already cooperating with Quantrill at this early stage. By the spring of 1863, though, leadership of the group had apparently devolved onto Bill Anderson, and he and his small band of followers soon ventured into Jackson County and fell in with the celebrated Quantrill.[3] Some of the veteran Missouri guerrillas had probably heard of Anderson, but for many of them it was likely the first time they had seen him.

A handsome man of average height and weight, the newcomer was "a fine military figure on horseback" with his dapper dress and long locks of black hair cascading to his shoulders. His chin jutted forward beneath a stubble of thick beard, and a sharp nose and high cheekbones highlighted his angular features. His eyes, deeply recessed beneath heavy brows, had a piercing stare that seemed to bore right through the other guerrillas without seeing. They were "small angry eyes" with "a peculiar gleam" that reminded one observer of "a sort of cross between an eagle and a snake."[4]

This new man named Anderson was quiet almost to the point of reticence, and although he seemed agreeable enough, the other guerrillas could not help but notice the "sneering smile" that played continually across his features.

Some of the tougher men no doubt greeted the newcomer with dubious frowns. Already hardened by more than a year of fierce guerrilla fighting, they were some of the most ferocious men in the country and had little to learn about the brutalities of war. How could this upstart from Kansas fit in with them? Little could they have guessed they were looking at the man who would soon become, in the words of Cole Younger, "the most desperate of desperate men."[5]

Anderson's first action of note with the Missouri guerrillas was his participation with Dick Yeager, one of Quantrill's "captains," in a daring raid deep into Kansas. About thirty guerrillas slipped across the border in small groups and rendezvoused just south of Council Grove on May 2, 1863. One band was known to have camped the previous night at Bluff Creek, for-

Guerrilla Chieftain William Quantrill, a photo made from a portrait.
—Used by permission, State Historical Society of Missouri

mer residence of the Andersons, and Bill Anderson was recognized as a member of Yeager's gang by area men who went out from Council Grove to parley with the bushwhackers.[6]

Yeager relinquished his design to plunder Council Grove and instead went fifteen miles west to the stage station and store at Diamond Springs, where the guerrillas killed the store owner and wounded his wife when she tried to protect him. They looted and burned the place and stole all the horses on the premises.

Continuing west on the Santa Fe Trail, the gang was intercepted by a large posse under a U.S. marshal. A dozen of the guerrillas were captured and turned over to Capt. John Stewart, former jayhawker and cohort of Quantrill before the war. On the way to Fort Riley, according to T. Dwight Thacher, loyalist editor of the *Kansas City Daily Journal of Commerce*, "the bushwhackers attempted to escape, when the guard fired upon them and the whole number were killed. A good riddance."[7]

The posse scattered the rest of Yeager's gang, and the guerrillas worked their way back toward Missouri in small bands, committing depredations along the way. At Rock Springs they riddled a furloughed Union soldier with bullets, and all along the Santa Fe Trail they terrorized citizens and stole horses and other property.

During the winter of 1862–63, Quantrill had made a trip to Richmond, Virginia, in quest of a Confederate colonel's commission and authority to raise a regiment under the Partisan Ranger Act. The guerrilla chieftain was thwarted in this mission but, nonetheless, acted briefly as colonel of a loosely organized "regiment" during the summer and fall of 1863. Some of his former men referred to him as "Colonel" even after the war, but his official Confederate rank was never higher than captain.

Despite Quantrill's hunger for recognition, he did very little during the spring and early summer upon his return from Richmond. Unlike the previous year, when he had personally led his men on virtually every adventure, his command split into bands that operated independently under his various captains and came together only on occasion. Quantrill himself was content to hole up in the Sni Hills with his runaway lover, Kate King, who took Quantrill's middle name, Clarke, as her surname and became his child bride.

Because he already had a small following, Anderson was made a lieutenant under Capt. George Todd in the loose, unofficial structure of the regiment.[8] During his summer tutelage with the veteran Todd, a man who had already earned a reputation as a fierce fighter, Anderson grew adept at ambush and probably got his first taste of regular warfare. Todd's command attacked and routed a company of Federals in mid-June at the southern edge of Westport. Fourteen Yankee soldiers were ridden down and killed with bullets through the head or heart. A few weeks later, Todd skirmished with Union troops at the present site of Lee's Summit.

Just as the captains under Quantrill often acted independently, so, too, did the lieutenants under the various captains break off at times from the main commands. Anderson was not the type to take orders from others for very long, and he frequently led his own small band in some separate action. Now, though, that he was affiliated with the most notorious gang of guerrillas on the frontier, bigger things were required of him. Anderson wasted no time in proving he could be just as murderous as the next fellow.

A *Lexington Union* article reveals that Anderson had become a notorious guerrilla leader by mid-July:

> Last Monday morning about twenty bushwhackers, under Anderson and Pool, passed through the German settlement in Freedom township, shooting, killing and murdering the Germans indiscriminately as they went. Four were killed and six or seven wounded. These men were plowing in their fields without arms.[9]

The editor of the *Union* goes on to rebuke Southern-sympathizing citizens for abetting such murder and rapine. His complaint shows what Union officials were up against, not just in Lafayette County but throughout western Missouri:

You may travel over every mile of this county, and visit every man personally in it, and he will tell you that he is opposed to all such work, and hopes the troops may catch the villains and kill them. Yet no man is hurt but those who are known to be Union men. There is a wrong somewhere. If the people are opposed to these bands, why are they not all treated alike? No, gentlemen, you willfully lie when you say you are enemies to the villains, and many of you daily come to town with loyalty on your lips and deceit in your hearts.

Anderson and Pool's raid into Lafayette County is also recounted in the official records in the form of a letter written by a private citizen named Sam Breitenbaugh to Brigadier General Ewing and dated July 15, 1863.[10] Breitenbaugh's account of the affair essentially agrees with the newspaper version except that Breitenbaugh makes the unlikely claim that, in addition to the four murdered men, a girl was also killed.

The German victims, the letter reveals, were members of the Union militia. In addition to those killed and wounded, one man was captured and paroled with orders to report to Colonel McFerran at Lexington in a prospective exchange of prisoners. By paroling the militiaman to McFerran, Anderson and Pool hoped to effect the release of a guerrilla named William Ogden, who was being held in Kansas. Another militiaman, named Colonel Childs, was also taken captive and was herded through the brush to be hanged. Dave Pool was on the verge of stringing the colonel up when some of his former friends among the guerrillas spoke up on the prisoner's behalf, and Pool spared his life, swearing, however, that he meant to kill fifty Union men in retaliation for the death of "Colonel" Ben Parker, a guerrilla leader who had been killed in Waverly two weeks earlier.

"This band," Breitenbaugh, reported, "is headed by one W. T. Anderson, who formerly lived in this place." The latter half of the statement is somewhat inaccurate. While Ogden and perhaps others of Anderson's men were from Lafayette County, there is no evidence that Anderson himself ever lived in the immediate area, except as a bushwhacker.

In late July, Quantrill's combined command rendezvoused near Lexington and contemplated an attack on the fortified Union installation there. Anderson, already making a name for himself as a brash fighter, urged the assault, but cooler heads prevailed and the perilous plan was abandoned.

Splitting with the main command after the rendezvous at Lexington, Anderson led a raid into Kansas on the night of July 31. Just beyond the border from Westport in Wyandotte County, he and a band of about twenty-five bushwhackers robbed a wagon train of wine, broke open several boxes, and took a black man prisoner. Then they headed down the Shawnee Road.

Captain Coleman of the Sixth Kansas Cavalry, stationed at Little Santa Fe, had somehow learned of the intended raid on the wagon train and sent word to Captain Harvey of the Ninth Cavalry at Westport to come out and help intercept the guerrillas. The Union pursuit, however, turned into a fiasco.

Arriving at the campsite of the wagon train about thirty minutes after Anderson's gang had departed, Harvey immediately gave pursuit and chanced upon Coleman's force coming up from Santa Fe. Coleman mistook Harvey's cavalrymen for the robbers and ordered an attack. Harvey formed his men into a line and fired upon the charging Federals, killing one man, but as soon as Coleman returned fire, Harvey's inexperienced fighters broke and ran. Coleman's Sixth Kansas chased the fleeing soldiers some distance before realizing the mistake.

Meanwhile, Anderson stopped at the house of Wright Bookout near Turkey Creek and called him to the door. When the man refused to come out, the marauders shot him dead.

At a crossroads known as the Junction, they came to the home of a loyalist named Saviers, whose son was a member of the hated Kansas Red Legs. The bushwhackers surrounded the stone house after the occupant let it be known that he planned to offer a stiff resistance. In the gun battle that followed, Saviers sustained an injury but also wounded a member of Anderson's band. During the commotion, the black man made his escape, and the guerrillas retired from the fray to seek an easier target.

Swinging northwest, they stole along the Kaw Valley and visited the home of a Mr. Johnson. Finding him absent, they plundered the home and insulted the man's wife "with their hateful tongues."[11] Next they robbed a Shawnee Indian named Bigknife and put his house to the torch. After burning yet another house, they came finally to the home of a Union man named Stephen J. Payne and shot him to death in the presence of his family.

The gang followed the Kansas River to the home where the Anderson sisters were staying, gathered up the girls, and hightailed it back to the border before a pursuit could be made. Crossing to the Missouri side, Anderson deposited his sisters with the Joe Gray family near Little Santa Fe.

The following day, Coleman searched the area for the bushwhackers who had pulled off such a daring raid less than four miles from the Union's Kansas City headquarters. The Yankee troops crossed into Missouri, where they came upon the guerrillas, killed four of the gang, and wounded several.

One of the mortally wounded bushwhackers clung stubbornly to his saddle after having been shot. As his horse pranced about aimlessly through the brush, the soldiers filled the rider with lead, but still he didn't drop. When the shooting finally died down, the dying man was found strapped to the saddle, apparently to keep him from falling if he went to sleep. Like several of his comrades, he was dressed in Federal blue.

Minus their four dead comrades, the rest of the bushwhackers scattered into the Missouri woods. Despite the scrape with Captain Coleman, Bill Anderson went into hiding after the Wyandotte County raid with his standing as a full-fledged guerrilla leader now secure.

CHAPTER FIVE

They Murdered My Sister

A network of civilian support sustained the Missouri guerrillas throughout the war. In unfriendly territory they compelled cooperation at the point of a gun if the need arose, but around Jackson County they usually didn't have to, because loved ones were eager to help. Girls like Mary and Josephine Anderson often made trips into Kansas City or surrounding towns to obtain supplies and learn information that might benefit their brothers and boyfriends in the bush. Upon their return home, the girls brought with them not only food and ammunition but also news about the enemy, which they hurried through the woods to the guerrillas' secret hiding places.

On June 9, 1863, the Union Army's District of Kansas was split into two commands. Brig. Gen. Thomas Ewing was named commander of the District of the Border, and Brig. Gen. James G. Blunt, commander of the old District of Kansas, was exiled to the District of the Frontier.

The District of the Border, headquartered in Kansas City, encompassed all of Kansas above the thirty-eighth parallel and the following counties in Missouri: Jackson, Lafayette, Cass, Johnson, Bates, Henry, and parts of Vernon and St. Clair. Believing that Blunt had been too lenient in dealing with pro-Southern people in the region, Ewing ordered the arrest and imprisonment of many of the female relatives of the guerrillas in order to cut off Quantrill's lifeline. The roundup of young women began.

Shortly after the first of August, a detail of fourteen Union soldiers was sent out to arrest Mary and Josephine Anderson. They found the Anderson sisters in the Gray home south of Westport. Also present were Mrs. Gray (nee Lucinda Mundy); her two sisters, Martha and Sue Mundy; her fourteen-year-old brother; and a neighbor girl named Mollie Grandstaff.[1]

After initially resisting the arrest, the Anderson girls asked for time to comb their hair and change clothes. Thirteen-year-old Martha "Mattie" Anderson decided voluntarily to go with her older sisters rather than be left alone and made preparations for the journey as well.[2] In the meantime, the young boy slipped away to alert the girls' brother, who, after his foray into Kansas, had camped not far away.

Anderson dashed toward the house, but the girls were already in custody outside the home as Anderson and his band arrived. The sisters were mounted behind three cavalrymen, whose horses were walking along a narrow lane bounded by a rock fence. As the soldiers approached the end of the lane, Anderson and two other guerrillas leaped over the fence and ran to the middle of the road.

Anderson promptly raised a double-barrel shotgun and fired over the heads of the squad. The two sides faced each other in a tense standoff. The soldiers told Anderson they would shoot the girls if he wounded the horses or any of the men, but even without the threat, Anderson dared not fire low for fear of hitting his sisters.

The Federal soldiers backed their horses away from the guerrillas in a careful retreat toward the other end of the lane. As Anderson and his men leaped back over the fence, each side fired once at the other, but no one was hurt. Then the rest of the Union detail came up to join the advance squad, and the girls were taken off without further incident. All seven young women at the Gray home were eventually loaded into a wagon and hauled to Kansas City.

Because so many young women had been arrested throughout the summer, the Union Hotel, which served as the primary residence for the Southern girls, could not house them all, and a three-story brick building in the 1400 block of Grand Avenue was pressed into service. The Anderson girls and a number of other young women were placed there.

The building was owned by the wife of renowned Missouri artist George Caleb Bingham, but he was away serving a term as state treasurer at Jefferson City and was not using the structure at the time. The vacant third floor had once been used as the artist's studio, and the bottom floor contained a grocery store. The girls were housed on the second floor, which had living quarters.

On August 13 the *Kansas City Daily Journal of Commerce* reported that General Ewing had been to St. Louis to obtain authority and make arrangements for the banishment of the families of Missouri guerrillas from the District of the Border. The news was bound to enrage Quantrill's men, but later that day, before a report of the plan could reach the guerrillas in the bush, a disaster struck that overshadowed even the proposed exile of loved ones. The building on Grand Avenue collapsed, taking the imprisoned young women down in a heap of brick and rubble.

Soldiers and citizens hurried to the scene, but they could not immediately reach the victims because of the huge cloud of dust that arose. Terrible moans and screams came from the rubble. A girl thought to be Josephine Anderson kept pleading for someone to take the bricks off her head, but she soon fell silent. A few girls who managed to free themselves stood crying and cursing the Federals. Finally the dust cleared, and onlookers began to dig through the ruins. Five lifeless bodies were dragged from the pile. Among the dead was fifteen-year-old Josephine Anderson. Her sister Martha, or "Janie" as she was often called, had two broken legs and a twelve-pound ball chained to her ankle. Her guards had shackled her earlier that morning as punishment for annoying them. She wailed that she could have jumped to safety through an open window if she had not had the steel ball around her ankle. The third sister, Mary, escaped with minor injuries.[3]

Another of the dead was Charity McCorkle Kerr, sister of guerrilla John McCorkle. She had been imprisoned along with her sister-in-law Nannie Harris McCorkle, widow of John and Charity's brother Jabez. Nannie Harris McCorkle was also a cousin of Cole Younger.

Also killed in the collapse were two sisters of another member of Quantrill's band. The fifth dead woman was known only as Mrs. Wilson.

An angry mob, estimated by one source at between three and four thousand people, gathered at the scene while the girls were still being dug out. Many in the crowd cursed or threatened the soldiers. When Maj. Preston Plumb, General Ewing's chief of staff, arrived, the people were in such a nasty mood that he summoned the headquarters' guard and ordered them to fix bayonets to prevent a riot.

A rumor immediately circulated that the collapse was a diabolical scheme orchestrated by the Yankees. Guards had deliberately weakened the building's foundation in order to murder the girls. In support of this claim, angry citizens pointed to the old merchant who kept his store on the first floor. All morning long prior to the collapse, they said, he had been frantically removing his stock of goods to the street with the help of guards.

Union military authorities only heightened the bitter feelings when they claimed that the young women had contributed to the downfall themselves by tunneling around the foundation in an attempt to escape.

There is no evidence to support either the Union's claim that the young women caused the collapse themselves or the contention of Southern-sympathizing citizens that military authorities deliberately undermined the building for the purpose of killing the girls. The truth seems to lie somewhere in between.

In the years since the war, the accepted explanation for the collapse has been that the structure was poorly built and maintained. The rear of the building extended into a ravine, where the walls of the foundation had been constructed with no excavation. The intention was to fill in the low ground around the walls with dirt after construction in order to give the back part of the building earth support, but this plan was never carried out. The rear room of the building, too, had never been completed and lacked a floor. Hogs that roamed free in Kansas City at the time went there to lie in the cool shade. Rooting in the loose dirt along the walls, they further weakened the structure. Also, Bingham had added the third floor of the building for his studio after the first two floors were completed. A foundation designed to uphold two floors was thus called upon to support three. A strong gust of wind has usually been cited as the immediate cause of the collapse.

Recent evidence, however, suggests that the Grand Avenue building was not poorly constructed and that the Union guards did, indeed, undermine its foundation. Their reason, though, was more mundane than the guerrillas believed.

One contemporary theory holds that, while the Southern girls were kept on the second floor, the basement or cellar of the building was used as a prison for women "of bad character." An adjoining building housed the guards, and they had cut away girders from the supporting columns in the basement and knocked three large holes in the common cellar wall in order to gain access to the prostitutes.[4]

Another, perhaps more credible, explanation is that the Union guards knocked out the wall simply to give themselves more living space.[5]

On August 14, the day after the prison collapse, the *Kansas City Daily Journal of Commerce* reported the tragedy with a matter-of-fact, one-paragraph statement:

> The large three-story brick building in the Metropolitan Block, McGee's Addition, owned by G. C. Bingham, Esq. and occupied for the last two weeks as a guard house, fell in yesterday afternoon, carrying with it the adjoining building south. There were in the building at the time nine women prisoners, two children and one man. Four women were killed; the balance escaped without fatal injuries.

The next day the newspaper corrected the body count and gave the names of victims.

When the guerrillas in the bush learned of the tragedy, they immediately believed the story that the collapse had been engineered by Federal authorities. Hadn't the Union already destroyed many of their homes and killed many of their loved ones? The young men of Quantrill thought the Yankees capable of any depravity. John McCorkle, whose sister died in the collapse, later called it "a foul murder" and "one of the most brutal and fiendish acts that ever disgraced a so-called civilized nation."[6]

Something snapped inside Bill Anderson when he heard the news. He had lost four members of his family in the space of four years. His brother killed in a clash with Indians. His mother struck by lightning. His father shot by a double-crossing Kansas judge. And now his sister deliberately murdered by the Yankee guards. All of them dead! In addition, two other sisters had been wrongly imprisoned, one of whom was gravely injured. In his mind, somebody had to pay.[7]

Anderson swore eternal revenge on all Unionists and, according to legend, thereafter carried in his pocket a silken cord in which he tied a knot each time he killed a man, the same way a gunfighter might notch his pistol. It is said he would go into battle frothing at the mouth and whispering Josephine's name.

There is no doubt Anderson was an accomplished killer even before the prison collapse, but afterward he became utterly ruthless. The news of his sister's death ripped from his soul the last shreds of humanity. Insane with hatred, he became in the words of historian Richard Brownlee "a homicidal maniac" who showed no mercy toward anyone who served or supported the Union.[8] From that day forward, he lived to kill.

Certainly not all the guerrillas were as directly affected by the prison collapse as Anderson, but nearly all had a litany of grievances to recite. Cole Younger spoke of how jayhawkers had plundered and burned his father's business and stolen his horses and how a detail under a Union captain, who was carrying out a personal grudge, had then ambushed and killed Mr. Younger while he was returning from a trip to Kansas City to report the raid on his property. Frank James told the story of how, shortly after he joined Quantrill, Union soldiers had tried to hang his stepfather, flogged his younger brother Jesse with a whip, and then arrested both his mother and stepfather.

Guerrillas who didn't have similar stories to tell invented them. Quantrill himself said his older brother had been killed by jayhawkers in Kansas, when in truth he didn't have an older brother. For many, though, the tales of Union abuse were legitimate, and the news of the Grand Avenue building reopened old wounds.

The death of the Southern girls in the collapse is sometimes cited as the main reason for the Lawrence massacre. McCorkle, for one, makes such a claim in the book *Three Years with Quantrill*. In fact, Quantrill had been planning the raid all summer and had met with his officers to disclose the plan a few days before the collapse, although some of the leaders balked at the idea. No doubt the collapse helped convince them, and the outrage of the guerrillas over the event may have contributed to the enormity that occurred at Lawrence eight days later.

Quantrill knew that if he were ever going to convince three hundred men to venture more than forty miles deep into enemy territory at the risk of being ridden down and annihilated by a superior force on the open plains of Kansas, now was the time. Lawrence was a symbol of everything the Missourians hated. It was a hotbed of abolitionism dating back to the days of "Bleeding Kansas." The town was even named after Amos Lawrence, sponsor of the New England Emigrant Aid Company, which had helped bring Northern settlers to the territory. Lawrence was the home of Jim Lane and other hated jayhawkers. The guerrillas, Quantrill told them, could get more revenge and more plunder there than anywhere else.

John N. Edwards, Quantrill's first biographer and chief apologist, has the guerrilla chieftain polling his leaders one by one:

"What is it, Anderson?" Quantrill is supposed to have asked.

"Lawrence or hell," Anderson replies, "but with one proviso, that we kill every male thing."

"Todd?"

"Lawrence, if I knew that not a man would get back alive."[9]

And so it goes. As Quantrill queries each man, each in turn voices his support for the attack on Lawrence. Whether such a formal polling ever took place is questionable, and the text of the conversation is surely fictional, as is much of Edwards' book. But the guerrilla chieftain did seek and obtain unanimity in devotion to the mission. Quantrill urged Lawrence, and Lawrence it was.

On August 18, four days after the collapse of the Grand Avenue building, General Ewing added another insult to the guerrillas' inventory of grievances when he issued Order No. 10, putting into effect the plan that had first been announced in the newspaper on the morning of the tragedy:

> Officers will arrest, and send to the district provost-marshal for punishment, all men (and all women not heads of families) who willfully aid and encourage guerrillas, with a written statement of the names and residences of such persons and of the proof against them. They will discriminate as carefully as possible between those who were compelled, by threats or fears, to aid the rebels and those who aid them from disloyal motives. The wives and children of known guerrillas, and also women who are heads of families and are willfully engaged in aiding guerrillas, will be notified by such officers to remove out of this district and out of the State of Missouri forthwith. They will be permitted to take, unmolested, their stock, provisions, and household goods. If they fail to remove promptly, they will be sent by such officers, under escort, to Kansas City for shipment south, with their clothes and such necessary household furniture and provision as may be worth saving.[10]

The guerrillas knew what the order meant. Their loved ones would have to leave the area with no more than they could carry with them. Coming so soon after the prison collapse, the decree was a bitter pill that further excited the guerrillas' wrath.

On the evening of that same day, Quantrill arrived with 150

men at the farm of Captain Perdee on the Blackwater River in northwestern Johnson County, a rendezvous point he had pre-elected, and the various captains showed up with their bands throughout the evening. Bill Anderson rode in with 40 men.

Some of the Missouri guerrillas still questioned the wisdom of undertaking the long, perilous march to Lawrence, but Anderson wasn't among them.

Chapter Six

I Have Glutted My Vengeance

On the morning of August 19, 1863, nearly three hundred guerrillas broke camp on the Blackwater and headed west, slowly feeling their way through a territory grown thick with Union soldiers.[1] They covered just ten miles during the day and stopped for supper near Lone Jack at the Potter farm. Here Quantrill addressed the assembled guerrillas, disclosing to the rank and file for the first time their destination and warning them of the peril involved in undertaking the march. "I consider it almost a forlorn hope," the chieftain said, "for, if we go, I don't know if anyone of us will get back to tell the story."[2]

Quantrill offered to let anyone who wished to leave the command do so without censure. Only a handful took him up on the offer.

After a brief rest, the guerrillas saddled up and rode through the night. At dawn of the 20th they stopped again, on the Grand River in Cass County, just four miles from the Kansas line. They rested here throughout the day and were reinforced by a band of about 50 men who had heard rumors of a major raid and rode in from Cass and Bates counties to join the frolic.

At midafternoon the guerrillas saddled up again, and the march to Lawrence began in earnest. At the Blue River, a hundred new recruits from northern Missouri under Confederate colonel John D. Holt ran across the guerrillas by accident, and the colonel agreed to go along with Quantrill to have his green troops "christened."

Holt's recruits brought the number of men under Quantrill to approximately 450, the largest guerrilla force ever assembled under a single command during the Civil War. It was a motley outfit.

The farm boys from the Grand River area and the raw recruits under Holt were mostly dressed in the drab butternut clothes of the day. They were unevenly mounted, and some were armed with just hunting rifles or shotguns. Most had no idea what they were getting into.

The veteran Quantrill men were dressed in Federal blue uniforms confiscated from the enemy or sported the peculiar "guerrilla shirt" lovingly embroidered by a wife or sister. Superior horsemen, they were mounted on the best animals in the West, and they were armed to the teeth. Most had at least two Navy Colt revolvers stuck under their broad leather belts, and some carried as many as six. Not all of them were hardened killers, but Bill Anderson and a few others like him were among the most deadly of men.

The guerrillas crossed the border below Aubrey, Kansas, where a company of Union soldiers under Capt. J. A. Pike was stationed. Shortly after Quantrill passed through, a frantic farmer who briefly had been held prisoner by the guerrillas rushed to Pike with the news. Pike dispatched an alarm to other Union commanders in the area but failed to pursue the guerrillas or to alert towns to the west that were likely targets for a raid.

Quantrill's march continued to Spring Hill, then swung northwest to Gardner. From there the guerrilla command followed the Santa Fe Trail for a few miles and came upon Benjamin O'Dell and his daughter on their way from Chicken Creek to Kansas City for winter supplies. Bushwhackers in the advance party relieved the old man of his bedding and his two-horse team.

O'Dell was standing there in fright and confusion when Bill

Anderson rode up and recognized his old Kansas neighbor. The two exchanged greetings, and Anderson promised to get the man's horses back but said the guerrillas needed the blankets. Anderson left and came back a few minutes later with one of O'Dell's horses and a second horse, but not the same one that had been stolen. Anderson told the old man to take the horse as a trade because it was the best he could do for him and also gave the man money to buy new bedding when he got to Kansas City.

By August of 1863, it was a rare instance when Bill Anderson spared a Unionist, and he knew the old man to be the strongest kind of Yankee. But O'Dell was an old acquaintance, and that made all the difference.[3]

Leaving the Santa Fe Trail, the guerrillas veered north along a faint trail that led toward Lawrence. The night was lit only by stars, and Quantrill, unsure of his directions in the dark, sent some of his men to a farmhouse to enlist a guide. After leading the guerrillas about a mile, the man was recognized as a former Missourian and shot to death for being a turncoat.

In similar fashion, eight more guides, impugned as abolitionists or dismissed for no longer knowing the road, were shot down over the next several miles to prevent them from sounding an alarm. At the small town of Hesper, twelve miles from Lawrence, a man was pulled from his home and immediately recognized by George Todd as Joseph Stone, a former Missourian who had caused Todd's arrest back in Kansas City at the start of the war. Todd was afraid that gunfire so near Lawrence might arouse neighbors to rush to town with an alert, so he told a new guerrilla whose loyalty was suspect that there was a simple way to prove his devotion. All he had to do was bludgeon Stone to death with the butt of a rifle. The young recruit stepped to the task with a verve that made even some of the veterans wince.

At Hesper, Quantrill started to recognize some of his old haunts and decided that no more guides were needed. Just in case, though, he snatched a young boy named Jacob Rote from the Stone place and put him on one of the guerrillas' horses.

At the community of Franklin, the first rays of sun streaked the eastern sky, and Quantrill ordered his men to rush on. Most of the guerrillas had slept little since breaking camp on the Blackwater almost forty-eight hours earlier, and some had even tied themselves in their saddles to keep from falling off their horses. They jolted awake, though, at the command and formed into columns of four. Outside the small town they broke into a gallop.

At a crest in the trail two miles from Lawrence, Quantrill paused to let the rear catch up and to send scouts ahead to reconnoiter the town. A few of the guerrillas, stunned by the size of the town and afraid that the element of surprise had been sacrificed to daylight, wanted to turn back. Quantrill told them to do what they wanted but that he was going to Lawrence. Without waiting for the scouts to return, he spurred his horse forward. To a man, the others followed, although some shook their heads in dismay, and one cried out that they were lost.

At the edge of town, two guerrillas spotted a man out in his barnyard milking a cow, broke away from the main column, and shot him. He was the Rev. S. S. Snyder, recruiting agent and lieutenant for the Second Colored Regiment. Snyder was the first victim of the day.

Here Quantrill gave an order, relayed by the captains, that under no circumstance was any woman or child, black or white, to be molested. Then he sent pickets to cordon off the town.

The rest of the guerrillas plunged on, overrunning a camp of white Union recruits at an open lot near the center of town. They knocked down tents, trampling some of the terrified soldiers under their horses' hooves. The ones who tried to flee were ridden down and shot. Seventeen of the twenty-two unarmed recruits were killed and the other five wounded.

Black recruits in a separate camp at the far end of the lot were alerted by the gunfire, and most managed to escape by hiding or dashing to the water of the Kansas River four blocks away.

At the Union camp, one of Anderson's followers, Larkin Skaggs, confiscated a U.S. flag and tied it to his horse's tail. Then he and the rest of the guerrilla command charged toward the business district with the flag dragging in the dirt. The horde of bushwhackers stampeded down Massachusetts Street, Lawrence's main avenue, firing revolvers left and right.

They pulled up in front of the Eldridge House, Lawrence's finest hotel, and all got quiet for a moment. Presently a man appeared at an upstairs window, waving a white bed sheet for a flag, and he identified himself as Capt. Alexander Banks, provost marshal of Kansas. He offered to surrender the hotel in exchange for a promise that the occupants would be protected.

Quantrill agreed and ordered a few of his men to stay with him at the hotel. The rest he dismissed with a final reminder to kill every man capable of carrying a gun. "Kill!" he shouted. "Kill and you will make no mistake!"[4]

While Quantrill and his squad put the hotel guests under guard and robbed them, the rest of the command took to the streets, plundering, burning buildings, and getting drunk on stolen whiskey. Anderson lingered at the Eldridge House long enough to relieve Banks of his military uniform before joining the melee.[5] Some of the rioters, emulating Larkin Skaggs, tied miniature American flags that they had looted from a store to the tails of their horses and rode up and down Massachusetts firing their pistols. Any male citizen foolish or unfortunate enough to appear on the streets was promptly gunned down.

A block from the Eldridge, Todd and Anderson's men surrounded the Johnson House, hangout of the hated Kansas Red Legs, and demanded that the guests come out. When no one emerged, the guerrillas took pot shots at the hotel windows. Several men leaped from the building, and they were shot as they hit the ground. The bushwhackers renewed their call for surrender, promising that they only intended to burn the hotel and that if the men would give themselves up, they would be spared.

Eight men trudged from the building and stood trembling before the bushwhackers. One of the men was ordered to turn over a pistol he had in his possession. As soon he handed the weapon to his captor, a second guerrilla shot him in the stomach. The victim sagged against Ralph Dix, the man standing beside him, and clutched Dix's arm in a death grip.

The faces of the other men blanched with horror, and some

fell to their knees, begging for mercy with outstretched hands. Dix's frantic wife, Getta, rushed up and cried, "Oh, my God, Ralph, have you given yourself up as a prisoner? Why did you do it? I know they will kill you."[6]

Dix, who had left his home only minutes earlier and crawled across the roof of a barbershop to reach the protective stone walls of the Johnson House, pled with his wife to intercede on his behalf. The sobbing woman did all she could, but the leader of the gang was unyielding. "I have killed seven 'red legs,'" he boasted "and I'll kill eight more."

The eight men protested that they weren't Red Legs, but the Rebels prodded them to their feet and drove them across the street toward the Methodist church. Despite the threats and curses of the guerrillas, Getta clung to her husband's arm, begging them at every step not to hurt him.

Finally her pleas softened the hearts of two of the bushwhackers, and they promised to spare Dix's life. The leader was not as charitable. "No, I won't let you take your husband away," he swore. "I'm going to kill every damn one of them."

As the party started toward Massachusetts Street, the murderous guerrilla kept trying to nudge Getta out of the way with his horse, but she fought off the horse's head with one hand while holding her husband's arm with the other. Then, as the group started to cross an alley, Getta tripped over a pile of rocks and lost her grip on Ralph's arm when she fell. Instantly, "this one villainous man" opened fire, killing Getta's husband first. Mrs. Dix tried to get back to her feet and reach her husband, but bushwhackers stampeding their horses down the alley right over the dead bodies sent her reeling toward Massachusetts Street.

While some of the guerrillas stayed in the downtown area throughout the morning, many broke into squads and roamed the residential areas, killing unarmed civilians in their homes. Bill Anderson and George Todd crossed a ravine into affluent West Lawrence and pulled from their pockets pieces of paper on which were listed the names of Kansas citizens who were special targets of the raid. Spies for Quantrill had helped compile the "death list," and the guerrilla chieftain had distributed copies to his captains. At the top of the list was Senator Jim Lane.

Lane, though, had made his escape at the first sounds of gunfire. Clad just in his nightshirt, he had jumped out of bed, raced through a cornfield, and hidden in a nearby ravine. Not finding Lane at home, the guerrillas had to content themselves with looting and burning his house. The senator's fancy ceremonial sword was among the booty taken. Although Jim Lane was the most hated of Kansans, the bushwhackers helped his wife save some of her possessions before putting a torch to the property.

Other prominent citizens in Lane's neighborhood were not as fortunate as the senator. Dr. Jerome Griswold, State Senator S. M. Thorpe, and newspaper editor Josiah F. Trask were lured out of Griswold's home with a promise of protection and then shot to death for walking too slowly as the guerrillas marched them toward downtown. Mayor George W. Collamore was also among the victims in West Lawrence. When the bushwhackers surrounded his home and demanded he come out, the mayor hid in a well beneath an attached building to escape the villains. He died from poisonous fumes when they fired the house.

Early in the morning, a squad of guerrillas arrived at the home of Gurdon Grovenor to burn the house. Mrs. Grovenor pled with the leader to spare the house, saying it was all the property she had. Finally the man relented and, as he drew his men off, swore a huge oath that the place would not be burned.

About an hour later, another party of guerrillas under a different leader showed up, intent on firing the house. Again Mrs. Grovenor begged that her home be spared, but this time her appeals seemed futile, for the gang appeared determined to burn the house regardless. Finally, the lady related the visit of the earlier gang, thoroughly described its leader, and said this man had vowed that her house would not be burned. The leader of the second party looked suddenly surprised. "If Bill Anderson spared your house," he exclaimed, "I should be ashamed to burn it!" He then turned with his whole squad and rode away without another word.[7]

I Have Glutted My Vengeance 45

Later during the massacre, Anderson presented himself at the Bullene residence, where Todd had set up his personal headquarters, and demanded something to eat. When the lady who waited on him rebuked the guerrillas for their outrageous behavior, Anderson reportedly replied,

> I had two sisters arrested in Kansas City by Union men, for entertaining Southern sentiments. They were imprisoned in a dilapidated building used as a guard-house. The building was known to be unsafe, and besides it was undermined. One night that building fell and my two sisters with three other ladies were crushed to death.[8]

Anderson paused a moment and then added, "Jennison has laid waste our homes, and your 'red legs' have perpetrated un-heard of crimes. I am here for revenge—and I have got it."

At approximately nine o'clock that morning, guerrillas placed as lookouts on Mt. Oread at the southwestern edge of town spotted the distant swirl of dust from a body of riders approaching Lawrence from the east. Union cavalry! The message was relayed to Quantrill, who ordered the guerrillas to assemble at a park in the south section of town for the retreat.

The Grovenor home, which Anderson had spared early in the morning, was located near the spot where the soldiers had been killed when the guerrillas first rode into town, and Anderson passed by the house again on his way to the rendezvous point. Mrs. Grovenor had apparently encountered a guerrilla more hard-hearted than Anderson, for her house was now in flames.

Anderson saw her standing in the yard and paused to strike up a conversation. He told the woman of the number of men he had killed that morning and inquired as to where her husband was. Mrs. Grovenor said he had been taken prisoner and carried away. In truth, the man was hiding in a cellar beneath the ell portion of the flaming structure, but the ruse worked and Anderson rode away.[9]

As the bushwhackers gathered to leave, Quantrill outfitted

Jacob Rote, the boy who had been compelled to pilot the guerrillas to Lawrence, with a new suit of clothes and sent the youngster on his way. Then he dispatched William Gregg to round up stragglers.

One man Gregg couldn't rein in was Larkin Skaggs. The thirty-two-year-old Skaggs was so drunk he could hardly stay in the saddle, and he was unaware that the other guerrillas were fixing to leave. He was still downtown, looking for a black preacher named Dudley Lee. Skaggs, a hard-shell Baptist preacher himself, was ranting that Lee was a runaway slave who belonged to him.

He finally gave up his search for Lee and went instead to the City Hotel, owned by Nathan Stone, an old acquaintance of Quantrill whom the guerrilla chieftain had protected throughout the morning. Earlier in the day, Skaggs had taken from Stone's daughter Lydia a diamond ring that Quantrill himself had given the young woman back in 1860 for having nursed him through an illness. Apprised of the theft by Lydia, Quantrill had forced Skaggs to return the ring and scolded him for disobeying orders not to bother the Stone family. Skaggs gave Miss Stone the ring back with a warning that she would be sorry for it.

Now he was returning to carry out the threat. Lydia, however, was not at the hotel, and Skaggs took out his frustration by setting fire to the structure. When Nathan Stone protested, Skaggs shot him dead.

Skaggs turned and rode off down the empty street. He paused to try to burn a woman's house and kill a man but failed on both counts. Finally the realization that he was the only bushwhacker left in Lawrence penetrated Skaggs' besotted brain, and he headed out of town to catch up with his comrades.

In his stupor, however, Skaggs rode in the wrong direction and was driven back toward Lawrence by a party of men in pursuit of Quantrill. At the edge of town he was riddled with bullets and scalped, and his body was dragged in the dirt behind a horse the same way he had dragged the Union flag. He was the only guerrilla killed in Lawrence, although Jim Bledsoe and a

Monument in Lawrence's Oak Hill Cemetery dedicated to the victims of the Lawrence massacre.

couple of new recruits under Holt were injured and placed in an ambulance for the trip back to Missouri.

As the retreating guerrillas started their march south, huge clouds of black smoke banked in the sky above Lawrence, and a river of blood flowed in the streets below. Between 150 and 200 men lay dead, victims of a four-hour orgy of slaughter.

Many of the guerrillas had not taken an active hand in the killing. The farmers from the Cass County area and the raw recruits under Holt served mainly as pickets. Even some of the regular guerrillas were appalled by the bloodbath and limited their activities to plundering and burning. Although he had given the order to kill, Quantrill himself protected the captives at the Eldridge House and a few other citizens he had known during his days in Kansas. Even the ferocious George Todd, despite the fact that his men did their share of killing, protected captives under his guard and saved the life of at least one man.

Enough, though, showed no such restraint. Bill Anderson claimed to have killed fourteen men, and as Edwards says, "the number was allowed to him."[10] Larkin Skaggs wasn't far behind, although he didn't live to brag about the count. Peyton Long, a Quantrill follower who later rode with Anderson, was said to have killed more than any other man. Eighteen-year-old Arch "Little Archie" Clement, a smiling assassin who would go on to become Anderson's right-hand man and chief executioner, also did murderous work, as did part-time Anderson disciple Frank James. William E. Connelley, Quantrill biographer who interviewed many ex-guerrillas, said that at Lawrence, "The band of Bill Anderson did more killing than that of any other captain."[11]

Anderson, perhaps more than any of the other guerrillas, went to Lawrence to slake a thirst for blood, and he did not stop until he had glutted his vengeance.

CHAPTER SEVEN

Quantrill's Sand Is Gone

Quantrill retreated south along the Lawrence–to–Fort Scott Road, burning barns and homes as he went. A few miles south of Lawrence, a group of bushwhackers went to the home of a Mr. Rothrock and compelled his wife to fix them breakfast. Upon learning that the old man was a Dunkard minister, one of the guerrillas declared, "Oh, we intend to kill all the damned preachers," and shot the man several times.[1]

Near Brooklyn at the intersection of the Santa Fe Road, however, Quantrill spotted a large force of Union soldiers angling across the prairie toward the guerrillas from the northeast. The time for murder and plunder was over. The goal now was just to get back to Missouri.

The Union pursuers were under the command of Maj. Preston B. Plumb, Ewing's chief of staff. The message of Captain Pike, commander at Aubrey, had reached Kansas City about midnight the previous evening. Plumb had correctly surmised that the guerrillas were Quantrill's command and had set off in pursuit with thirty infantrymen mounted on plug horses.

He arrived at Olathe about daylight and was there reinforced by a company under the command of Lt. Cyrus Leland Jr. Conferring with the junior officer in an effort to determine

Quantrill's whereabouts, Plumb spotted a great cloud of smoke rising in the western sky and exclaimed that Quantrill was in Lawrence. The combined forces struck northwest across the prairie toward the town.

Beyond Captain's Creek they met another Union company, under Capt. Charles F. Coleman, the same officer who had chased Anderson after his raid on the Shawnee Road the night of July 31. Stationed at Little Santa Fe, Coleman had answered Pike's alarm by hurrying to Aubrey, where he took command of Pike's company. South of town, he picked up Quantrill's trail and followed it to Gardner before losing track of the guerrillas. In the early morning of the 21st, he spied the "smoke from the burning of Lawrence and pressed on as fast as our jaded horses would permit."[2]

Near the Wakarusa River, Plumb and his reinforcements saw a trail of smoke rise in the sky south of Lawrence. Quantrill was burning houses during his retreat from the town! Again the Union command left the trail and struck across the prairie in pursuit. Soon the Rebels were in sight!

In the meantime, Senator Lane had organized a poorly armed band of civilians and trailed Quantrill out of Lawrence on plow horses and exhausted animals the bushwhackers had exchanged for fresh mounts. At Brooklyn, the ragtag outfit caught up with a small party of guerrillas torching a home, and Lane's men put the stragglers to flight.

They followed Quantrill down the Fort Scott Road, hanging on the guerrillas' left flank. Alarmed at the pursuit, the retreating bushwhackers lightened their loads, abandoning pack horses and strewing plunder across the prairie. Soon Plumb's Union army came up to join Lane, and the chase was on.

Around noon, Plumb's advance cavalry rode up on the rear of the guerrillas, who had stalled trying to get through a narrow lane that passed between two cornfields. Plumb ordered a charge, but George Todd rallied the stragglers and countercharged, repelling the attack. A few miles beyond the cornfields, the guerrillas came to East Ottawa Creek and had to pause long enough at the crossing to allow Plumb's advance to come up again. This time Quantrill himself led the counterattack. He and his rear guard drove the Federals all the way back to the cornfields, giving the rest of the guerrillas time to cross the creek.

Beyond the crossing, Quantrill left the Fort Scott Road and angled toward Paola. All afternoon, the two sides fought a running battle across the prairie in scorching August heat. Each time the Yankees came up, the rear guard of the guerrillas checked the attack long enough to let the main body under Quantrill get far to the front. Then the rear guard galloped to join the main body.

At dusk near Paola, the bushwhackers finally broke contact with their pursuers. The Federals paused to rest their spent animals, but Quantrill pressed on through the night, drawing steadily closer to the safety of the Missouri woods. Near dawn of the 22nd, they crossed the border only a few miles from where they had entered Kansas thirty-six hours earlier. After a brief skirmish with Missouri militia, the guerrillas scattered in all directions.

Had the invasion of Lawrence not resulted in the murder of innocent civilians, it would have been deemed an extraordinary success and Quantrill praised as a superb tactician. From a strictly military standpoint, the raid was a remarkable accomplishment. Quantrill had led 450 men almost fifty miles deep into enemy territory, caught the town unaware, and made it back to Missouri with few casualties despite being pressed hard by Union forces during most of the retreat.

Reaching Missouri, though, did not guarantee safety for the bushwhackers, as many were hunted down and slain on the spot. Just inside the state line, Quantrill was forced to abandon the ambulance containing Bledsoe and the two raw recruits. Union soldiers found the carriage hidden in some woods, and the two green recruits began to beg for mercy. Bledsoe told them to quit carrying on so. "We are not entitled to mercy!" he exclaimed. "We spare none and do not expect to be spared!"[3]

With the Federal soldiers was a Delaware Indian named White Turkey, who had chased the guerrillas all the way from Lawrence. After the soldiers executed the three Missourians, the Indian took out his knife and scalped them. Andy Blunt, one of Quantrill's captains, happened upon the scene a few hours later. After studying the bodies a moment, he turned to his companions. "We had something to learn yet, boys, and we have learned it. Scalp for scalp hereafter!"[4]

All told, Union soldiers killed as many as a hundred or more Missourians in the area around Jackson County during the weeks that followed the Lawrence raid. Not all, of course, were Quantrill men. Some had not been to Lawrence at all, and a few were not even Southern sympathizers. In their zeal to avenge the horror of Lawrence, Union soldiers did not always take pains to determine guilt.

Official Union reaction to the atrocity was swift and stern as well. On August 25, General Ewing issued Order No. 11 requiring all citizens living in Jackson, Cass, and Bates counties and part of Vernon County, except those residing within one mile of a Federal army post, to establish their loyalty and move to a military station within fifteen days or to leave the district. Under terms of the order, all grain and hay remaining in the district and not brought to military stations within fifteen days would be destroyed.

Cass County had approximately ten thousand people at the time of Order No. 11. Fifteen days later, only six hundred remained. Altogether, more than twenty thousand people were displaced from western Missouri by the order. Barns and homes as well as grain were put to the torch, and the area became known as the "Burnt District."

Meanwhile, Federal troops scoured the hills and woods for bushwhackers still in the area, but Quantrill and most of his "old men" eluded the intense search, frustrating Federal officers to no end. The complaint of Col. Bazel F. Lazear in a September 10 letter to his wife is typical: "Quantrell is in here yet with some three hundred men but they are so scattered that it is hard to find them."[5]

Loss of civilian support and increased Federal patrols, though, made guerrilla warfare difficult, and Quantrill decided not to tarry in the area. Although cold weather was a month away, he sent word for the guerrillas to meet on September 30 at the Perdee farm on the Blackwater River in Johnson County for the march south to winter quarters. About 450 men answered the call and assembled at the old rendezvous point. Included among the number were the recruits under Holt, who had been unable to leave the area because of Union vigilance. On the morning of October 2, the march to Texas began.

Four days later, the guerrillas struck the Fort Scott–to–Fort Gibson Road, and the advance guard under Dave Pool captured two Union soldiers driving a wagon loaded with lumber near Spring River. The prisoners told Pool they were headed to Fort Blair, a Union outpost that was still under construction at Baxter Springs, Kansas. Pool killed the captives, sent word back to Quantrill of the fort's existence, and then rode forward to investigate. A company under William Gregg came up to reinforce Pool while Quantrill took the main body of guerrillas to a stand of timber north of the fort, with plans to attack from that direction.

The Union fort consisted just of one row of barracks made of logs and an area behind the barracks partially enclosed by earthen and log embankments. Garrisoned at the fort were about 150 soldiers under Lt. James B. Pond, but sixty of them were away in a foraging party. Most of the remainder had stacked their arms in the entrenchment and clustered at a kitchen area south of the fort for the noon meal. Pond was in his tent to the west of the fort.

Pool and Gregg charged in on the unsuspecting camp as the soldiers were eating. They opened fire, cutting the Yankees off from their weapons and the protection of the entrenchment. Pond and his men, though, dashed between horses through the ranks of the guerrillas and reached the fort with only a few casualties. Some of the bushwhackers galloped right into the dugout, and a brief but furious firefight ensued, with screams of men piercing the air and bullets whizzing in all directions and thunking against the earthen embankments.

When the bushwhackers retreated and formed in a line for another attack, Pond sprang to a twelve-pound mountain how-

Monument to the victims of the Baxter Springs massacre in the town's national cemetery.

itzer that rested just outside the embankment. Though unfamiliar with the weapon, the lieutenant managed to get off several rounds of artillery that landed near the guerrillas, throwing their ranks into momentary confusion and discouraging another assault on the fort. Gregg went off to find Quantrill, and Pool dropped back out of range of the menacing howitzer.

Gregg discovered Quantrill and the main body of guerrillas north of the fort in a standoff with about a hundred Union soldiers. Quantrill was lined up on the eastern side of the Fort Gibson Road at the edge of some woods, and the Federals were stretched out on the open prairie, facing him from the other side.

The Union force was a convoy under Gen. James G. Blunt, former commander of the District of Kansas who had taken over the recently formed District of the Frontier. Blunt had departed Fort Scott on the evening of October 4, taking with him as an escort one company of the Third Wisconsin Cavalry and one company of the Fourteenth Kansas, about a hundred men in all. Also in the party were fourteen members of the brigade band and a few civilians.

Upon approaching the fort at Baxter Springs, Blunt had paused to let the convoy close ranks and to bring the band to the head of the march for the purpose of making a showy entrance. He was separated from the fort by a stand of heavy woods and did not hear the sounds of battle raging less than a mile away. He was just getting ready to resume the march when Quantrill emerged from the woods to his east. Blunt assumed that the guerrillas, dressed mainly in Federal blue, were some of Pond's cavalry on drill or a welcoming party from the fort sent out to greet him.

The first inkling that he was wrong came when he saw leaders of the guerrillas riding up and down the line in an apparent attempt to organize the formation. Blunt ordered his escort to form into a line as more bushwhackers came out of the woods until the Federals were outnumbered by about three to one. The guerrillas started forward at a walk and commenced firing when they were two hundred yards away.

Two green Yankee cavalrymen broke and ran, followed by

eight more. Seeing the confusion in the Yankee line, Quantrill shouted, "Charge!"

The whole Union force turned and scattered across the prairie in mad flight, and the "battle" turned into a horse race that the Federals were doomed to lose. Mounted on superior animals, the bushwhackers rode the Union soldiers down one by one and shot them at point-blank range like frontiersmen killing a herd of buffalo.

Some of Anderson's band did not participate in the chase but contented themselves instead with gathering up plunder from the Union convoy that was strewn across the prairie. This action caused animosity between the men of Quantrill and Todd and those of Anderson. Already a rift was developing between the two camps.

In all, about ninety Union soldiers were killed, including seven shot at the fort, and another twenty wounded. Quantrill's own report placed guerrilla casualties at just three dead and three wounded, but the actual figure was slightly higher.

Quantrill, mistakenly believing that General Blunt was among the dead (actually, he managed to escape on a fleet horse), reportedly got drunk on the general's own whiskey and rode about the battlefield strewn with bodies, declaring, "By God, Shelby could not whip Blunt. Neither could Marmaduke. But I whipped him!"[6]

Another bushwhacker who got rip-roaring drunk on the confiscated whiskey was a sixteen-year-old Anderson follower named Riley Crawford, whose mother had brought him to Quantrill after the boy's father had been killed by Union soldiers the previous January. After feasting on rations taken from Blunt's supply train, Crawford stumbled over to a fallen Union soldier and struck the body with the broad side of a sword. "Get up, you Federal son of a bitch!" the drunken bushwhacker mocked.[7]

To Crawford's astonishment, the soldier jumped to his feet. He had been merely feigning death and, when prodded with the sword, falsely assumed his charade had been found out. The

Marriage certificate of William T. Anderson and Bush Smith from a microfilm copy at the Sherman (Texas) Public Library.

young guerrilla promptly pulled his revolver and accomplished the man's final exit.

After the bushwhackers regrouped, Anderson and Todd urged another assault on the fort, but Quantrill declined, saying it was too risky and not worth the loss of any of his men's lives. The ever-calculating Quantrill may have been under the influence of drink, but the whiskey hadn't eclipsed his discretion. Late in the afternoon, the guerrillas skirted the fort and resumed their march south.

Four days later, near the Arkansas River, they encountered a party of about a dozen Federal Indians and, in Quantrill's own words, "brought none of them through."[8]

On October 12 the guerrillas arrived in the camp of Confederate general Douglas Cooper on the Canadian River, and the next day Quantrill wrote a report to General Price of the action at Baxter Springs. After resting at Cooper's camp a few days, the bushwhackers went on to Texas and established winter quarters on Mineral Creek about fifteen miles northwest of Sherman.

The disintegration of Quantrill's command began almost immediately. Some of the men were sickened by what they had been a party to during the summer and fall campaign, and even the bloodthirsty experienced an emotional letdown after the visceral highs excited by the slaughters at Lawrence and Baxter Springs. According to William Gregg, the guerrillas no longer felt the sense of purpose that had previously united them. A cloud of gloom set in as reports of Union victories in the East made the war look more and more like a lost cause. The bushwhackers quarreled over division of the spoils from Lawrence and other summer raids.

In November, Gregg, Cole Younger, and about forty other "old, tried, and true veterans," as Gregg called them, who had been with Quantrill almost from the beginning, left the command.[9] The remainder grew increasingly raucous and hard to control.

Confederate general Henry McCulloch, commander of the Subdistrict of North Texas, tried to rein in the bushwhackers by assigning them various tasks. Detailed to chase renegade Comanche Indians, the Missourians gave up after a week when they realized they had more than met their match in horsemanship. Told to round up Confederate deserters and Union jayhawkers, the guerrillas, to McCulloch's bewilderment, killed as many as they brought in. Ordered to break up stills in the area, Quantrill and his men managed to smash just one, because they rather enjoyed the products of the stills themselves. In frustration, McCulloch tried to get Quantrill reassigned to southern Texas, but Quantrill had no disposition to make the trip.

On Christmas Eve, many of the bushwhackers got drunk in Sherman and shot up the town. Quantrill had to come in from his camp on Mineral Creek to restore order. A week later, on New Year's Eve, some of the men were at a dance in Sherman, and others who hadn't been invited tried to crash the party. The two sides argued, and again Quantrill had to be summoned to prevent violence.

After the new year, Anderson announced his intention of marrying a girl from Sherman named Bush Smith. Quantrill reportedly opposed the wedding and urged Anderson to wait until the war was over, thus aggravating the growing friction between the two men. Over Quantrill's objections, Anderson and his closest followers left Mineral Creek and took up quarters in Sherman. The two camps traded threats, and Anderson set up guards in anticipation of a showdown in the streets of Sherman with his old chieftain. The fight never materialized, and the wedding went on as scheduled. Some of the Quantrill men even attended the ceremony.[10]

The rowdiness of the bushwhackers escalated, though. Not only did their drunken behavior in the streets of Sherman continue, but they were also suspected of robbing and killing citizens in the area, including a Confederate major named Butts. Throughout the winter, Confederate authorities tried to get the Missourians to quit their bushwhacking and to enter regular service.

In early March, Quantrill finally acceded in part to official wishes. After talking to General Price, he returned to the

Mineral Creek camp with instructions to reduce the outfit to just eighty-four men and to send the rest into regular service. In the resulting reorganization, Anderson's band was again absorbed into Quantrill's command.

Quantrill was to serve as "colonel" of what was now a nonexistent regiment and was to exercise control over all the guerrilla bands of western Missouri. Todd was made captain of the company. Anderson was elected first lieutenant, and Fletch Taylor became second lieutenant.

The new organization, though, fell apart almost as soon as it was established, and Anderson made his final break with Quantrill.

A man named Morgan, who had belonged to Anderson's old gang, stole a bolt of cloth from one of Quantrill's men and had a pair of pants made from it. Upon learning of the theft, Quantrill sent a squad to escort Morgan across the Red River into Indian Territory (Oklahoma), where he was turned loose with the warning that he would be killed if he came back into Texas. Morgan disregarded the warning, came back across the river, and murdered a farmer. Quantrill sent a squad out to kill Morgan.

At about the same time, Quantrill also got wind that four bushwhackers, including Fletch Taylor, had been responsible for the murder of Major Butts. Quantrill arrested the four and sent a request to General McCulloch that Taylor be court-martialed. Before he could deliver the prisoners to Confederate headquarters, though, they escaped with the complicity of the guerrillas who were detailed to guard them.

Quantrill called all the men together in an attempt to restore order to the disintegrating command. He told them that those guilty of crimes against the property of Texas citizens who admitted their guilt and promised not to repeat the offenses would be protected and allowed to stay in the command. Those who did not admit such depredations, however, and whose crimes were later proved against them would be expelled from the command and turned over to authorities. He added that any man who didn't like his style of commanding was welcome to mount his horse and leave.

Bill Anderson, furious over Quantrill's execution of Morgan and failure to protect Taylor, stepped forward. He said he hadn't broken any laws of Texas but added that he didn't want to belong to any such outfit. He rode out of camp followed by twenty men and headed to Sherman.[11]

After pondering the defection awhile, Quantrill decided that he didn't care whether Anderson quit but that he wasn't going to let him take twenty good men with him. He gathered the remaining bushwhackers and followed the deserters to the home in Sherman where Anderson's wife was staying. Surrounding the house, though, the guerrillas found it empty except for Bush Smith and a few other women. Someone had warned Anderson that Quantrill was on his trail, and he and his men had gone on to Bonham, where General McCulloch's headquarters were located.

Fletch Taylor had reached Bonham ahead of Anderson. He admitted to McCulloch that he had killed Butts but told the general that he did so under orders from Quantrill. When Anderson arrived, he backed Taylor up and added that Quantrill and his men had committed all sorts of crimes in Texas.

Upon hearing these accusations, McCulloch summoned Quantrill to Bonham. The general told the guerrilla chieftain that Taylor was in custody and that Quantrill should bring all his witnesses against the lieutenant. Quantrill must have known that Anderson and Taylor had had the general's ear and that McCulloch was looking for any pretext to discipline him. Nonetheless, Quantrill saddled up and rode to Bonham, taking all his men except twelve, who stayed behind with Todd to guard the camp.

Quantrill arrived about noon on March 26, 1864, and tied his horse to a hitching rail outside the City Hotel. He told his men to stay mounted and ready for trouble. Then he went inside the hotel and climbed the stairs to the second floor, where McCulloch's headquarters was located.

McCulloch informed Quantrill of Taylor's charges and placed the chieftain under arrest. Then, adopting a conciliatory manner, he said he would accept Quantrill's parole until a trial could he held, and he invited the guerrilla leader to accompany him to dinner.

"No, sir!" Quantrill stormed. "I will not go to dinner. By God, I don't care a goddamn if I never eat another bite in Texas!"[12]

McCulloch shrugged, placed Quantrill under guard, and went to dinner alone. Within minutes, though, the wily guerrilla leader got the drop on his two guards and raced into the street. Disregarding orders, most of his men had dismounted and were visiting with some of Anderson's boys who had happened by. Although the guerrilla leaders were at odds, friendships yet existed among the two commands.

"Mount your horses, men!" Quantrill cried. "We're all prisoners here."

He and his men sprang to their saddles with a shout and galloped out of town toward Sherman. He sent a messenger on a fleet race mare back to the Mineral Creek camp with word for Todd to gather up all the ammunition he and his men could carry and meet him on the Bonham to Sherman road. From there, Quantrill planned to swing north and cross the Red River at Colbert's Ferry.

Upon learning of Quantrill's daring escape, General McCulloch immediately sent Colonel J. Martin of the Texas militia after the fugitive with orders to bring him back dead or alive. Anderson and his men joined the chase as an advance for Martin's regiment. Occasionally they closed to within skirmishing distance of their old comrades, but no one was hurt in the halfhearted exchange of gunfire.

Before Quantrill and Todd could rendezvous, Martin came up on Quantrill and forced him to abandon the road about five miles east of Sherman and swing north toward the ferry. Meanwhile, Anderson retired from the chase and rested with about twenty men in some woods beside the road near Bodark Creek. Todd crossed the creek and, spotting Anderson, formed his men in some timber on the opposite side of the road.

The two bands exchanged a few shots, with the result that

one man on each side was slightly wounded. Then they paused to trade insults.

"If you're not a damn set of cowards," yelled Anderson, "come out in the open and fight like men."[13]

"You have the most men," Todd called. "If you're not a goddamn set of cowards, come in here and take us out."

The haphazard gunfight resumed, but for the reckless bushwhackers it was more sport than battle. They popped away at each other like boys firing play pistols in a mock shootout, but no further damage was done except to the bark of a few trees. No one relished the idea of actually killing an old buddy. At last Todd, hearing the sounds of distant gunfire to the north, slipped away along the timber of the creek to find Quantrill.

Todd caught up with Quantrill, and the command made it across the Red River and out of the jurisdiction of General McCulloch. Martin called off his chase and returned to Bonham.

During the night, some of Anderson's men crossed the river and sneaked into the Quantrill camp, where they kidnapped one of Quantrill's men and then tried to inflict the ultimate indignity by stealing Old Charley, the chieftain's horse. The animal created such a commotion kicking and whinnying, though, that the would-be horse thieves had to give up and make their escape.

Anderson eased back down into Texas, obtained a commission as a captain from General Price, and waited for warmer weather.[14] He was on his own now, having thrown off the yoke of the more celebrated Quantrill. Most folks back in Missouri had never heard of Bill Anderson, but as soon as he could make the trip north, that figured to change.

CHAPTER EIGHT

I Had Them to Kill

Because of the dispute with Confederate authorities, Quantrill and Todd started north sooner than planned, but Anderson tarried in Texas awhile longer and didn't arrive back in Missouri until late spring. On the march north, his band passed through the northwestern edge of Greene County, where the bushwhackers, many dressed in Federal uniforms, came upon a Union man named Joseph Cooper, who had served briefly in the Enrolled Missouri Militia. Impressing the young man as a guide, they took him across the line into Polk County, shot him, and inflicted upon the body "mutilation of such a horrible and revolting character as not to be described."[1]

When Anderson reached the vicinity of the Missouri River, he found that, because of Order No. 11, Jackson County offered less civilian support than it had in the past. Brig. Gen. Egbert B. Brown, commander of the newly organized District of Central Missouri, had let a few Southern sympathizers back into the region upon promises of loyalty, but he was determined to prevent the bushwhackers from regaining a stronghold in their old stamping grounds. The border area was thick with Union scouting parties.

The stepped-up Union vigilance, though, merely forced the

guerrilla captains to move their field of operations farther east. Spotted in Lafayette County in early June, Anderson showed up in Cooper County in central Missouri on the morning of the 4th with a band of twelve men and went on a tear.[2] Dressed mainly in Federal pants and greatcoats, they first visited the Bell Air community in the central part of the county. They there robbed a man named John Tucker and accosted Mr. and Mrs. James Hutchinson in their home. One of the gang reportedly choked the recalcitrant Mrs. Hutchinson to make her relinquish her money.

The marauders next stopped at the home of Nathaniel Leonard in the same community and found him even more obstinate than Mrs. Hutchinson. He refused to surrender his premises until after he was shot in the hand during a brief gun battle and the gang set his house on fire. The bandits then robbed him of clothing, jewelry, and three horses before impressing his son Leverett Leonard as a guide and setting out northwest toward Pilot Grove.

Not far from the village, they paid a call at the home of Mr. William H. Mayo. A former Quantrill guerrilla named Higbee and a partner had tried to rob Mayo two weeks earlier, and Mayo had scared them off with a shotgun, one of the guerrillas supposedly having been hit by a scattering of birdshot.[3] It is unclear whether Higbee was along with Anderson now, but circumstances suggest that the guerrillas were determined to look Mayo up and exact revenge.

Not finding him at home, they demanded to know where he was, but his wife refused to tell them. They then inquired at the Negro quarters and were eventually informed that Mr. Mayo had gone to Pilot Grove to the post office. The brigands robbed Mayo's premises of goods and other valuables and stole a horse, then started for Pilot Grove.

Along the way they robbed several other citizens, and, as they approached the village, Anderson sent one of the gang ahead to reconnoiter. Upon reaching the post office, the point man pulled out his revolver and ordered the occupants to come outside. About ten or twelve citizens had already begun trooping from the office when the rest of the gang rode up.

Anderson lined the men up and demanded their money, watches, and other valuables, but Mayo refused to hand over his watch and turned to go back into the post office. The guerrillas fired on him as he tried to escape, wounding him in the leg, and one of the gang remarked that he guessed Mayo wouldn't be shooting at them now.

Mayo then dashed through an orchard to try to make his escape. A Mr. Brownfield, who had tarried inside the post office, heard the shots out front and supposed all the citizens were being fired upon. Bolting out the back door with his pistol, he caught up with Mayo in the orchard, but the two parted as soon as they saw a guerrilla chasing them on horseback. The bushwhacker quickly overtook the unarmed Mayo and shot him through the forehead, killing him instantly.

The horseman then took up pursuit of Brownfield and was soon joined by two comrades, but Brownfield gained the cover of a thicket. Making a stand in the brush, he exchanged a brief fire with the guerrillas, who quickly retired to seek easier targets rather than risk injury or death in an attempt to flush him out.

The three guerrillas returned to the post office, where the work of plunder was winding up. The bushwhackers loaded their horses down with loot, the leader let it be known that his name was Anderson, and the band started off to the west in the direction of Buffalo Prairie.

At Longwood in Pettis County during the late afternoon of the same day, the gang robbed several citizens and, according to one report, killed an old man named Woolfork north of the community. A company of State Militia pursued the robbers but was two hours behind them at Longwood and soon called off the chase.

Continuing west, Anderson cut telegraph wires north of Pleasant Hill near the Cass-Jackson county line on June 11. Early the next morning his gang, having joined up with Dick Yeager, held up the Warrensburg-Independence stage a couple of miles east of Big Creek in Johnson County, near Archie Clement's hometown of Kingsville. The guerrillas stole the mail, scattered it on the ground, and robbed one of the passengers of between two and three hundred dollars.

A bushwhacker named Clement, very likely a brother or cousin to Arch Clement, had been captured in the area and shot to death by Federal troops less than two months before, and Little Archie was no doubt itching for a chance at revenge.[4] He got it just minutes later when the guerrillas came upon a fifteen-man scouting party of Missouri State Militia in the same vicinity where they had robbed the stage.

The partisan force of fifty men, clad in Federal blue, rode up on the Union rear. When Cpl. Joseph Parman, leader of the squad, shouted a challenge, the guerrillas only increased their speed. The small squad formed in a line and tried to mount a defense, but the charging guerrillas rode right through the line with pistols blazing. The bullets from Anderson and Yeager's bands were, in Parman's own words, "falling like hail."[5] Some of the cavalrymen tried to run but were ridden down and shot. A few tried to surrender and were likewise killed.

Only Parman and two of his men managed to escape to the woods with their lives. The bodies of the other twelve lay strewn along the road for half a mile and at the edge of the brush. The guerrillas, who suffered no casualties of their own, stripped the bodies of everything valuable, including uniforms, then took a scalp from one of the dead.[6]

Later the same day, a large detachment from Parman's First Cavalry followed the trail of the bushwhackers north and found them in the woods near Lone Jack in extreme southeastern Jackson County. After a brief skirmish in which one guerrilla was wounded, Anderson slipped away into the rugged Sni Hills.

Moving east, on June 13 his band attacked a wagon train with thirty men of the First Cavalry twelve miles south of Lexington in Lafayette County. Union losses were nine men killed, two wagons burned, and twelve mules shot.

Of the twenty-three Union soldiers killed by guerrillas in the Central District of Missouri during a ten-day period in the middle of June, Anderson accounted for all but two with his attacks on Parman's squad and on the wagon train.

Anderson's band had returned from Texas striking hard and often, and Union officials came under increasing attack for failing to drive out the partisans. On June 14, the *Kansas City Daily Journal of Commerce* complained that "no man of known and open loyalty can safely live for a moment" and claimed that "the rebels hold possession of the country."

In response to such pressure, Gen. William S. Rosecrans, commander of the Department of Missouri, in concert with Gen. Samuel R. Curtis and the Department of Kansas, mounted a campaign to try to eradicate the bushwhackers. Kansas troops under Col. Thomas Moonlight left Aubrey, Kansas, on June 16 and swept through Jackson and Cass counties and then through the Sni Hills north to the Missouri River. Marching and countermarching until June 20, the Kansas force drove most of the bushwhackers farther east but failed to capture or kill a single one.

In Missouri, General Brown took up the chase. Patrols under his command managed to kill twenty-seven guerrillas (few, if any, belonging to Anderson) during mid-June, but the crackdown failed to eradicate the bushwhackers. Scattering into small bands of three or four men or moving still farther east, the guerrillas merely lay low for a while.

The fact that nearly all guerrilla bands wore Federal uniforms by the summer of 1864 complicated the Union task of driving out the bushwhackers. Intricate signs and countersigns were adopted by Union officials in an effort to combat the duplicity, but guerrilla leaders like Anderson often learned the signs almost as soon as the orders instituting them were issued. The guerrilla deception made life especially perilous for private citizens, who, when asked by soldiers where their sympathies lay, never knew for sure to whom they were talking.

A few days after the assault on the wagon train, Anderson was still camped in east-central Lafayette County on Davis Creek, not far from the site of the attack and just north of the German settlement he and Dave Pool had raided the previous summer. Within a week, though, he had moved to the Missouri River, where on June 24 his band attacked a steamboat named the *West Wind* a few miles above Lexington in the area of Wellington. A single guerrilla hailed the boat, threatening to shoot if it didn't stop. When the pilot refused to heed the call and maneuvered instead toward the far shore, a number of other bushwhackers, concealed in the brush along the bank, blasted away at the boat, firing from two to three hundred shots with little effect. The *West Wind,* on its way from St. Louis, made it on up the river to St. Joseph without casualties.

On July 1, Anderson kidnapped the postmaster at Wellington and two other Union citizens in response to the arrest and death sentence of a guerrilla named Erwin. Anderson threatened to kill the hostages if Erwin was executed. In response, General Brown temporarily countermanded the execution order but also directed that six prominent Southern sympathizers in the Wellington area be seized and held until the three Unionists were released.[7]

Anderson, though, had already turned the hostages loose as soon as the messenger to Brown had been dispatched. He and his gang moved down the river, where he menaced another steamer a few days later. On July 4 about fifteen of the gang rushed down to the Waverly Landing below Lexington and tried to board the *Live Oak* on horseback while it was lying at dock receiving freight. Seeing the charge, the watch officer cut the cable and shoved the boat away from the bank just in time to prevent the guerrillas from boarding.

The frustrated bushwhackers fired a volley of between 150 and 200 shots at the retreating vessel, mainly at the pilot house. The watch officer was wounded during the barrage, and one horse was killed. The guerrillas claimed to be regular Confederate soldiers under Captain Anderson of General Shelby's command and insisted that all they were after was some government freight and a soldier who was supposed to be on board.

After failing in their design to board the *Live Oak,* the guerrillas spruced themselves up and repaired to a studio "uptown" to pose for photographs. After the brief interlude at the "picture gallery," though, they apparently went back to the business of bushwhacking. Just a few hours after the attack on the *Live Oak* at Waverly, the steamer *Post Boy* was fired upon as it passed the same location.[8]

Still in the Lexington area, Anderson momentarily put

down his guns in favor of a pen. On July 7 he sent four letters to the town's two newspapers. The letters are literate in style, but the text shows a mind crazed with hatred and a puerile sense of omnipotence. The tone is sometimes threatening, sometimes playful, but always cocky.

In the first letter, addressed to the editors of the town's two newspapers and indirectly to area citizens, Anderson responded to recent editorials urging civilians to openly resist the bushwhackers:

> Mr. Editors:
> In reading both your papers I see you urge the policy of the citizens taking up arms to defend their persons and property. You are only asking them to sign their death warrants. Do you not know, sirs, that you have some of Missouri's proudest, best, and noblest sons to cope with? Sirs, ask the people of Missouri, who are acquainted with me, if Anderson ever robbed them or mistreated them in any manner. All those that speak the truth will say never. Then what protection do they want? It is from thieves, not such men as I profess to have under my command. My command can give them more protection than all the Federals in the State against such enemies. There are thieves and robbers in the community, but they do not belong to any organized band; they do not fight for principles; they are for self-interest; they are just as afraid of me as they are of Federals. I will help the citizens rid the country of them. They are not friends of mine. I have used all that language can do to stop their thefts; I will now see what I can do by force. But listen to me, fellow-citizens; do not obey this last order. Do not take up arms if you value your lives and property. It is not in my power to save your lives if you do. If you proclaim to be in arms against the guerrillas I will kill you. I will hunt you down like wolves and murder you. You cannot escape. It will not be Federals after you. Your arms will be no protection to you. Twenty-five of my men can whip all that can get together. It will not be militia such as McFerran's, but regulars that have been in the field for three years, that are armed

with from two to four pistols and Sharps rifles. I commenced at the first of this war to fight for my country, not to steal from it. I have chosen guerrilla warfare to revenge myself for wrongs that I could not honorably avenge otherwise. I lived in Kansas when this war commenced. Because I would not fight the people of Missouri, my native State, the Yankees sought my life, but failed to get me. Revenged themselves by murdering my father, destroying all my property, and have since that time murdered one of my sisters and kept the other two in jail twelve months.

But I have fully glutted my vengeance. I have killed many. I am a guerrilla. I have never belonged to the Confederate Army, nor do my men. A good many of them are from Kansas. I have tried to war with the Federals honorably, but for retaliation I have done things, and am fearful will have to do that I would shrink from if possible to avoid. I have tried to teach the people of Missouri that I am their friend, but if you think that I am wrong, then it is your duty to fight. Take up arms against me and you are Federals. Your doctrine is an absurdity and I will kill you for being fools. Beware, men, before you make this fearful leap. I feel for you. You are in a critical situation. But remember there is a Southern army, headed by the best men in the nation. Many of their homes are in Missouri, and they will have the State or die in the attempt. You that sacrifice your principles for fear of losing your property will, I fear, forfeit your right to citizenship in Missouri. Young men, leave your mothers and fight for your principles. Let the Federals know that Missouri's sons will not be trampled on. I have no time to say anything more to you. Be careful how you act, for my eyes are upon you.[9]

In the next letter, addressed to Colonel McFerran, commanding officer of the Union post at Lexington, Anderson discussed his attacks on Parman's squad and on the wagon train. Although he may have overstated his own role in the skirmishes, his tally of Union soldiers killed is remarkably close to the actual number:

Colonel McFerran:

I have seen your official report to General Brown of two fights that have taken place in Johnson and La Fayette Counties with your men. You have been wrongfully informed, or you have willfully misrepresented the matter to your superior officer. I had the honor, sir, of being in command at both of those engagements. To enlighten you on the subject and to warn you against making future exaggerations I will say to you in the future to let me know in time, and when I fight your men I will make the proper report. As to the skirmish I had with your men in Johnson, I started to Kingsville with fifty men to take the place, but before I arrived there I discovered a scout, fourteen or fifteen of your men, on the prairie some half a mile distant to my left. I immediately gave chase. They fled. There were not over eight of my men ever got near them. They did not surrender or I would not have killed them, for I understood that Company M were Southern men; they sent me that word. I ordered them to halt and surrender. I was astonished to see them refuse after sending me such word. One of their lieutenants even planned the assassination of General Brown and the taking of his headquarters but I refused to commit so foul a deed. But they refused to surrender and I had them to kill. I regret having to kill such good Southern men, but they are fit for no service but yours, for they were very cowardly. Myself and two men killed nine of them when there were no other men in sight of us. They are such poor shots it is strange you don't have them practice more. Send them out and I will train them for you. After that I came down near Burris' camp with twenty-five regulars all told, belonging to the Kansas First, some of my first men. I understood that Burris was anxious to give me a thrashing. Not wishing to lose more than twenty-five men at one time, I thought I would try him with the aforesaid number, but while I was waiting for him to come out from camp, that I might devour him or be devoured, forty-eight of your men coming from Lexington with three wagons had the audacity to fire on my pickets, and very imprudently asked me to come out of the bush and fight them. I obeyed reluctantly. They dismounted and formed on a hill. I formed under their fire under the hill and charged. They fled and I pursued. You know the rest. If you do not, I can inform you; we killed ten on the ground and wounded as many more. Had all of my men done their duty we would have killed thirty of them. Farewell, friend.

The Burris mentioned in the preceding letter was a Kansas officer with whom Anderson had had previous skirmishes and, in the guerrilla leader's words, one of Colonel McFerran's "petty hirelings." The next letter was a playful note addressed directly to Captain Burris:

To Burris:
   Burris, I love you; come and see me. Good-by, boy; don't get discouraged. I glory in your spunk, but damn your judgment.

In his final letter, Anderson ranted against the death sentence of Erwin and the incarceration of Anna Fickle, a young woman who was awaiting trial for conspiring along with Andy Blunt and others during the previous winter to break a guerrilla named Hinton out of jail at Lexington:[10]

General Brown:
   I have not the honor of being acquainted with you, but from what I have heard of you I would take you to be a man of too much honor as to stoop so low as to incarcerate women for the deeds of men, but I see that you have done so in some cases. I do not like the idea of warring with women and children, but if you do not release all the women you have arrested in La Fayette County, I will hold the Union ladies in the county as hostages for them. I will tie them by the neck in the brush and starve them until they are released, if you do not release them. The ladies of Warrensburg must have Miss Fickle released. I hold them responsible for her speedy and safe return. General, do not think that I am jesting with you.

Area of Bill Anderson's operations.

I will have to resort to abusing your ladies if you do not quit imprisoning ours. As to the prisoner Ervin you have in Lexington, I have never seen nor heard of him until I learned that such a man was sentenced to be shot. I suppose that he is a Southern man or such a sentence would not have been passed. I hold the citizens of Lexington responsible for his life. The troops in Lexington are no protection to the town, only in the square. If he is killed, I will kill twenty times his number in Lexington. I am perfectly able to do so at any time.

Anderson signed the letter "Yours, respectfully, W. Anderson, Commanding Kansas First Guerrillas. He then attached a postscript asking that the Lexington editors please publish his letters and that other newspapers copy them. Instead, they were turned over to General Brown, who forwarded them to General Rosecrans "as a curiosity and specimen of a guerrilla chief's correspondence."

Anderson never got around to tying women up in the brush and starving them, but his willingness to make such a threat shows the twisted depths of his rage. He did not carry out his threats against the citizens of Lexington either, but he more than made up for the omission elsewhere. Leaving Lafayette, Anderson went on a savage rampage in neighboring counties.

On July 12 he followed the Missouri River east from Waverly with twenty-two guerrillas, looking for a boat to cross the river.[11] Just inside Saline County, Anderson spied a skiff on the far bank and sent two volunteers, Thomas Bell and Jesse Hamlet, to retrieve it. Bell tired or cramped in the middle of the river and drowned, but Hamlet made it across and brought the skiff back. The bushwhackers crossed the Big Muddy a few at a time, holding their horses by the reins and swimming them behind the boat.

The guerrillas landed on the north bank about six that evening in an area of Carroll County near Wakenda known as "the Gourd," a Union stronghold where many of the citizens were current or former members of the state militia. Mounting their horses, the bushwhackers quickly came upon four men, including a furloughed Union soldier named Neet, on their way to a schoolhouse for a meeting being organized for the protection of citizens from bushwhackers.

At first the men mistook the blue-clad partisans for Federal cavalrymen, but they quickly realized their mistake when the gang opened fire, killing a man named Hartgrove. The other three dashed for the brush. Neet was wounded in the shoulder and a ball whizzed through his hat, but he managed to make his escape with the other two men.

On down the road, the guerrillas met two more loyalists. Fooled by the blue uniforms, the pair admitted that they, too, were on their way to the militia meeting. The men were shot down for their candor. A third man was found plowing in his field nearby and was gunned down for refusing to reveal the politics of his neighbors.

Hiram Griffith, the next man Anderson came to, was also in a field, working behind a plow. Discovering the true identity of the guerrillas, Griffith defiantly insulted their leader. Smiling "Little Archie" Clement threw the offending farmer to the ground, slit his throat from ear to ear with a bowie knife, and left him floundering in a pool of blood.

Griffith and the other victims were robbed of money and clothes, and then the bushwhackers set off again. Visiting homes in the neighborhood, they terrorized women and demanded to know the whereabouts of the menfolk, but the resourceful ladies lied or refused to answer.

The murder of the five men in "the Gourd" had been the work of just an hour, but with darkness approaching, the gang decided to move on. Besides, there would be more men to kill on down the road.

The bushwhackers impressed local citizens as guides and rode rapidly east toward the Rock Ford, where Anderson planned to make his getaway across the Grand River into Chariton County. Along the way the gang stopped at a mill on Big Creek, where they found eighteen-year-old Solomon Baum, a Confederate sympathizer. They struck the lad with their pistols and kidnapped him.

Beyond the mill near Snow Branch, Anderson asked the kid whether he was a Union man, and Baum, assuming the guerrilla leader to be a ruffian Yankee, said that he was. The bushwhackers promptly took a rope from the saddle of one of their guides and started to hang the young man from a nearby tree. With a noose around his neck, the hapless Baum realized his mistake and pled for his life, vowing that he wasn't a Union man at all and would have long ago been in the Confederate army except for uncontrollable circumstances.

Anderson listened impassively to the boy's petition, then grew tired of toying with him. "Oh, string him up; goddamn his little soul, he's a Dutchman anyway." [12]

The bushwhackers did as they were told and left the corpse hanging from the tree as they rode away. Not far from the branch they came to the home of Cyrus Lyons, who was out in his yard, digging a well with the help of two neighbors named Edwin Matthews and John Henry. Inside the home were Lyons' three children and his gravely ill wife.

Anderson called Lyons over to the fence. "Why ain't you in the service?" he demanded.

"I do belong to the militia," Lyons said.

"Well, why in hell ain't you out trying to drive out the bushwhackers? Didn't you know they were in the country?"

Like the others before him, Lyons believed he was talking to a Union soldier. He responded that he had been in Captain Calvert's company, had always tried to do his duty, and was ready to serve again if he was needed.

"Well," Anderson barked, "I guess you've done enough. I am Bill Anderson, by God." He jerked out his pistol and shot Lyons dead.

Some of the other guerrillas leaped their horses over the fence and killed Matthews and Henry. Then as they looted the pockets of their victims, the bushwhackers roared with laughter and joked about the trick they had played on the "three damned milish."

Alarmed by the gunfire, Lyons' ailing wife dragged herself from her bed and crept on hands and knees across the floor to the door in an effort to reach her husband. Meanwhile, the bushwhackers rode off to find their next victim.

They came to the home of two men named Hume and robbed them of clothes, money, a horse, and a revolver. They threatened the wife of one of the men that they would kill her husband if she did not supply them with food and other items they demanded. Near Rock Ford the guerrillas kidnapped a man named Jenkins, whom they took with them across Grand River into Chariton County.

As soon as an alarm was raised, Captain Calvert, commander of the company to which Cyrus Lyons had belonged, came out from Carrolton and struck the trail of the bushwhackers but turned back at the ford, having gone, according to the *History of Carroll County,* "quite as far as was desirable or prudent."

The *Columbia Missouri Statesman* reported the news of Anderson's raid with a warning that "The Devil is let loose in Chariton and Carroll counties with scarcely three feet of chain to his neck."[13] Apparently Captain Calvert wasn't eager to tangle with the devil.

Anderson's foray through Carroll County was the beginning of a three-and-a-half-month warpath. Quantrill had gone into hiding in June with Kate Clarke in Howard County, and by mid-July, Todd was lying low in the Sni Hills. Anderson, though, took up the slack, slashing back and forth across the counties north of the river in an almost nonstop killing spree.

After the Carroll County raid, his gang stole several horses the next day in western Chariton and brutally beat two men who were members of the home guard. On the 14th they stopped a mail hack near Salisbury, killed Capt. Henry Snider of Jackson County, robbed the other passengers, and cut up the mail.

Afterward the guerrillas continued east and crossed into Randolph County. Early on the morning of July 15, they were on the road outside the county seat of Huntsville. Bill Anderson was headed home.

CHAPTER NINE

Things I Would Shrink from If Possible to Avoid

The Anderson gang rode into Huntsville about dawn.[1] Their leader sent a few men to picket his old hometown while the rest of the bushwhackers took possession of the business district. Some went to Sauvinet's Hotel and demanded that the landlord show them to his guests' rooms while the bulk of the gang began robbing citizens on the street and breaking into stores. A safe containing the county treasury was dragged onto the sidewalk from Morehead's store and broken open while a clerk at Mitchell and Blunt's drug store was forced to produce the keys to a safe that was used as a general depository for citizens. (The town had no bank.)

Tad Austin was asleep in the upstairs room of a house on the main street and was awakened by the commotion below. When he arose and poked his head out the window to see what was going on, two bushwhackers spotted him and called him into the street. Hurrying outside, he was told to go see the guerrillas' leader and to "be damned quick about it."[2] The two waved their guns toward a man on horseback a block or so away at the edge of the courthouse yard.

As Austin raced up to the leader, he was puzzled to see the horseman start toward him holding out his hand. "Hello, Tad," the rider said. "How are you getting along? Awfully glad to see you. How is all the folks?"

Austin could hardly believe his eyes. It was Bill Anderson, his old school chum. The two men shook hands, and Austin returned the guerrilla chief's greeting. Not knowing what a desperate fellow his old pal had become, Austin chatted amicably with Anderson awhile before Bloody Bill rode off to another part of town to direct the activities of his gang.

Meanwhile, the bushwhackers at the hotel accosted the lone guest, a man from St. Louis named George Damon. They robbed him at gunpoint, dragged him from his room, and marched him into the street. In front of Morehead's store, where some of the bushwhackers were still occupied in prying open the safe of the county treasury, Damon was surrounded by angry guerrillas who accused him of being a Federal officer and pointed to the U.S. belt buckle he wore as evidence. Anderson rode up, pulled out his Colt, and leveled it at the man.

Tad Austin, standing nearby, rushed over to intercede on behalf of his fellow prisoner. "For God's sake, Bill, please don't shoot that fellow. He's not a soldier; he's just a traveling man and never hurt anybody."

Anderson dropped his arm and appeared ready to let the poor fellow live. In the moment of tense silence that followed, though, Damon suddenly made a dash for freedom. Anderson wheeled and fired as the fugitive raced down the street along the plank board. Several members of the gang chased after him and opened fire as well. "Now damn you, stand when we tell you!" one of them shouted as the man fell wounded.[3]

Damon struggled to his feet and ran across the street and behind some horses toward the hotel where he had been staying. Anderson rode up and discovered the wounded man trying to scale a fence to reach the rear entrance of the building. He shot the man again, and Damon fell back into the yard, calling for water. When Mr. Sauvinet, the landlord, started to minister to the dying man, Anderson warned the hotel owner to leave Damon alone or he would shoot him, too.

Later, though, the man managed to crawl into the hotel under his own power, and some citizens came to Anderson and asked permission to fetch a doctor for the gravely injured Damon. "Is he still alive?" the guerrilla chief snarled as he turned to two of his men. "Go and finish him."

When the two bushwhackers went to the hotel to carry out their leader's order, Mrs. Sauvinet told them the poor man was going to die anyway and begged them not to shoot him anymore. "Why!" one of them exclaimed. "We would shoot Jesus Christ or God Almighty if he ran from us."

Seeing no signs of life, one of the villains put his head down to the man's chest to listen for a heartbeat. Hearing none, he took a ring from the finger of the corpse and slipped it on his own finger. Then the two tramped off to report the news of Damon's demise to their leader.

Near the end of the gang's two-hour stay in Huntsville, Anderson sent two messengers with a sack of stolen money to Tad Austin with instructions to let Austin remove that portion of the money belonging to him. Over ten years before, Tad's father Henry, who had fared better in the California gold mines than Anderson's father, had given the Anderson family $300 in gold dust upon the men's return to Missouri. Letting Tad recoup his share of the stolen money was apparently Bill's way of repaying the family debt, but Austin balked at the thin gesture of remission and told the two men he wasn't sure just how much of the money was his.

"Oh, that don't make any difference," one of the guerrillas declared. "Just hit something that will about cover your stuff and take it. We've got plenty."

After Austin dug out a few hundred dollars to cover his loss, the Anderson gang was still left with over $40,000 in money and another $3,500 worth of plunder taken during the raid. They mounted up and rode out of town on the Renick road. About six miles south of Huntsville, they stopped at the home of a farmer, struck him on the head with a pistol, and stole two of his horses before resuming their flight.

Ten miles south of town, a company of the Ninth Cavalry Missouri State Militia, which had been sent out from Sturgeon in pursuit, intercepted the guerrillas on the Fayette road. A running battle ensued over the next four miles, and one of the bushwhackers was shot. Mounted on superior horses, though, they soon outran the Yankees' jaded nags, leaving the road on which the chase had occurred strewn with ribbons, silk, and other loot from the Huntsville raid.

The guerrillas continued south and rested in the Perche Hills of western Boone County with plans to cross the river near Rocheport, which Anderson acclaimed his "capital" because of the many Southern sympathizers in the area. On the early morning of July 18, the gang rode into the village and announced, according to the July 22 *Columbia Missouri Statesman*, that, although they were thieves, they didn't think they would steal much from Rocheport, because it appeared the place had already been "pretty well cleaned out before their arrival." Besides, they added, they "didn't want to rob anymore no how," since they already had all the loot they needed. As evidence, they showed off purses crammed with greenbacks taken at Huntsville.

Unable to find the small boats supposed to be lying on the river near Rocheport, the guerrillas fired about thirty shots into the passing *War Eagle* in an attempt to force the steamer to stop and cross them to the other side. The *War Eagle* returned fire, passed on down the river, and two miles below Rocheport relayed information of the attack to another steamer coming up the river with cavalry aboard. The troops landed at Rocheport and surrounded the small town, only to discover that Anderson had already fled. After a token pursuit, the Yankees called off the hunt.

Drawn by tales of Anderson's exploits, brash young Missouri Rebels flocked to the guerrilla leader throughout the summer. Sixteen-year-old Jesse James joined the gang to follow in the footsteps of his brother Frank. Jim Cummins, another recruit during the summer of 1864, later expressed a sentiment typical of the newcomers: "Having looked the situation over I determined to join the worst devil in the bunch." Cummins added that, although Quantrill was fierce, "he was nothing to compare with that terrible Bill Anderson, so I decided it was Anderson for me."[4]

With the ranks of the gang swollen to sixty-five, Anderson roamed back into Randolph County and marched into Renick on the morning of July 23. The guerrillas robbed stores and tore down telegraph wires. After relieving the North Missouri Railroad agent of his valuables, they burned the depot and stated their intention to attack the train later that day at Allen. They recruited into the gang two local boys named Marney and Briggs and then headed out of town on the north road.

The train approached to within three miles of Allen, where a lady whose home the bushwhackers had passed flagged it down and warned the conductor of the impending attack. The train went back to Sturgeon to secure a guard of soldiers before proceeding.

Meanwhile, the gang struck Allen about noon and attacked a squad of forty troops of the Seventeenth Illinois Cavalry and the Missouri State Militia under Lt. Ebenezer Knapp, who had barricaded themselves in the train depot with barrels of salt and bales of hay as fortification. Unable to do much damage against the entrenched soldiers, the guerrillas, according to the July 29 *Columbia Missouri Statesman,* "amused themselves during the 'siege' by killing the horses" of the troops, which had been left tied outside the depot. After about an hour of fighting, a company of Enrolled Missouri Militia, who had been telegraphed for at the outset of battle, arrived by train from Macon City to reinforce Knapp and drive off the bushwhackers.

Anderson gathered up his wounded, left two comrades dead in the street, and fled east into the woods toward the Huntsville road. Three more bushwhackers, including the two new recruits, were killed during the brief Union pursuit. Yankee casualties were one man wounded and sixteen horses killed.

Anderson camped that night about three miles southeast of

Huntsville in a neighborhood where he had lived as a child during the late 1840s. The next day, July 24, Knapp and his squad of forty soldiers, reinforced by a party of sixteen civilians, went out in pursuit of the bushwhackers. The advance guard encountered the guerrillas on the Fayette road and quickly fell back with the main column. The bushwhackers immediately charged "with great fury."[5]

Knapp ordered his men to dismount and form in a line, but the first volley from the enemy threw the Union stand into a tumult. Not one of the Yankee horses had ever been under fire, and, in the words of the August 5 *Columbia Missouri Statesman,* "the confusion that followed such a charge as Anderson's men could make, may be imagined." The green animals bucked and snorted or bolted away, and most of the men fled to the woods in a panic.

A few stood their ground long enough to fire several shots at their attackers, killing one guerrilla and wounding Anderson himself. Two Federal soldiers, John Daniels of the Illinois Cavalry and John Nichols of the Missouri State Militia, were killed.

After the battle the bushwhackers caught and shot twenty-one of the Union horses, and vicious "Little Archie" Clement scalped the two dead soldiers in a bizarre manner. A round piece of skin "about the size of a Mexican dollar" was cut from the forehead of Daniels, and a larger slice of skin was stripped from the center of Nichols' forehead to the area of his left temple.

Then Clement or some other semiliterate bushwhacker scrawled the following note and pinned it to the collar of Daniels' coat:

> You come to hunt bushwhackers. Now you ar skelpt.
> Clenyent skept you.
> Wm Anderson

Plainly the note and the July 7 letters to the Lexington papers were not written by the same person. Either Anderson merely dictated rather than wrote the letters, or else one of his

Arch Clement, Anderson's right-hand man, photographed in uniform.
—Used by permission, State Historical Society of Missouri, Columbia

men must have scratched the note and appended his leader's name to it to ensure that the Anderson gang got due credit for the atrocity. If Arch Clement wrote it, he was unable even to spell his own name, but that's entirely possible, since the author was also unable to spell a simple word like "are" or even to misspell "scalped" consistently.

Meanwhile, Anderson carried his dead comrade to a neighboring house and left $35 with the occupant with orders to see to a decent burial of the corpse. Upon his return to the area of the skirmish, he allowed a party of civilians from Huntsville, under a flag of truce, to retrieve the remains of the two Union soldiers.

The bodies had been draped to hide the outrages committed upon them, and according to the *Columbia Missouri Statesman*, "When the bloody faces of the men were uncovered, an expression of horror involuntarily escaped the lips of those who looked upon them." The newspaper concluded, "Such a savage deed could only be perpetrated by such men as Anderson has under him."

After the Renick fight, Anderson raced northeast into Monroe County. He passed through Middle Grove on July 25 and left that evening in the direction of Paris. The Union army, seeing a rare opportunity to annihilate the band, was hot on his trail. Gen. J. B. Douglass, commander of the Eighth Military District headquartered at Sturgeon, sent several dispatches on the 26th vowing to put one hundred of his best mounted men on Anderson's track "until they kill or disband him."[6] Douglass reasoned that, because many of Anderson's men were strangers to north central Missouri, they would not easily be able to scatter and rendezvous at a designated point in normal guerrilla fashion and were, therefore, more likely to stay together.

Douglass' superiors concurred. Within four days, Gen. Clinton B. Fisk, commander of the District of North Missouri, had 650 men scouring a three-county area north of the river with orders to "follow Anderson's gang day and night until the villain is exterminated."[7]

Anderson, though, stayed one step ahead of the pursuit.

After leaving Middle Grove, he swung north, bypassing Paris, and galloped into Shelby County. On July 26 he struck Shelbina, where his gang, thirty-five strong, "raised the devil," robbing and plundering indiscriminately.[8]

Immediately upon riding into town, Anderson accosted a banker named Taylor at gunpoint, called him a "red-headed son of a bitch," and demanded that the man hold his horse. According to the *History of Monroe and Shelby County*, the banker "became at once a very efficient groom."[9] The guerrillas then called all the citizens into the street, forced them to line up, and proceeded to relieve them of their money and other valuables, despite the fact that many of the townspeople held Southern sympathies.

From the stores the Rebels took all manner of goods and notions, including ladies' and infants' wear. Some of the rowdy bushwhackers adorned their hats and clothing with ribbons or threaded them into the manes and tails of their horses.

After about three or four hours, the guerrillas fired the train depot with flammables they had stolen from the drug store and headed out of town. According to the county history, "They were not requested to remain longer!"[10]

East of Shelbina the guerrillas sent the station at Lakenan up in flames and then burned the 150-foot Salt River bridge on the Hannibal and St. Joe Railroad, seriously disrupting the transportation of Union troops in northern Missouri. They also burned the water tank and set a house near the bridge ablaze.

Southwest of the bridge, the bushwhackers stopped at the home of a citizen named Saunders and demanded dinner. While there, two guerrillas got into an argument over a watch that had been stolen in Shelbina. One of them shot the other one dead, and Saunders was obliged to dig the man's grave. Leaving the Shelbina area, Anderson dipped back into Randolph County, where he was reported on the 28th near the small village of Milton. On the morning of the 30th he went to the home of Lt. Col. A. F. Denny, the local militia commander, about two miles from Huntsville. He put a rope around the neck of the colonel's elderly father and hung him up until he was almost dead. In an attempt to draw the citizen soldiers of Huntsville into a trap, Anderson sent a Negro man into town with a message of the old man's plight, and, according to the August 12 *Columbia Missouri Statesman*, "it was with difficulty that the Colonel could be prevented from rushing to the rescue of his father." Mr. Denny was finally let down before he choked to death, and he trudged into Huntsville that afternoon with the rope still around his neck.

About this time, Anderson split his command into two bands. Most of the bushwhackers stayed around Huntsville and Randolph County under the command of Bill's brother Jim. On July 31 this contingent kidnapped thirty-two boys and young men from a church service in northwest Randolph and told the prisoners to step forward if they would be willing to fight for the South. The eight Union men who refused were subjected to various indignities, such as being stripped of clothes. Two were then whipped, four had their heads shaved, and two were made to kneel and pray under threat of execution.

Meanwhile, Bill Anderson led a party of about twelve guerrillas east with plans to rendezvous with Fletch Taylor in Clay County. He raced across Chariton and on the morning of Monday, August 1, crossed the Grand River into Carroll County near the mouth of Big Hurricane Creek. The guerrillas captured a citizen named William Darr, impressed him as a guide, and continued west.

During the ride, according to the *History of Carroll County*, Anderson lectured his prisoner on "the shortcomings of professed 'southern' men in Missouri who ... were rendering great service to the Federals by keeping on friendly terms with them." Such dubious Southerners, Anderson claimed, "ought to all go to bushwhacking and neither ask or give mercy." Otherwise, they were "no better than Yankees."[11]

Anderson asked Darr where he might find members of the militia who were not currently on active duty, and the captive replied that there were some who lived on Hurricane Creek and some on Big Creek. "By God," Anderson raved, "I'd like nothing better than to go over there and clean them up." According to the county history, "Mr. Darr had some difficulty in persuading him to forego his pleasurable mission."

Soon the guerrillas met Isaac W. Dugan, an ex-militiaman, on horseback and forced him to turn around and go with them as well. The gang amused themselves by prodding Dugan's horse with sticks, causing the skittish animal to kick wildly.

The bushwhackers stopped at the farm of Mary Mitchell in Hurricane Township and demanded lunch.[12] Besides the widow Mitchell, three other women were at the home—a daughter-in-law, Mrs. Caroline Mitchell; an unmarried daughter, Miss Susan Mitchell; and a married daughter, Mrs. Nancy Calvert, who had a newborn baby. While the women busied themselves carrying out the order to prepare a meal, the guerrillas turned their horses loose in the yard and fed them with oats that Dugan was forced to procure. After eating, some of the bushwhackers entertained themselves playing on a violin. Others tried to converse with the ladies while still others, worn out from their ride, fell asleep in the front yard.

Meanwhile, a party of about twelve citizens, who had organized a few miles to the east in hopes of rescuing Darr and Dugan, followed the bushwhackers and accidentally discovered them at the Mitchell farm. They left their horses, sneaked on foot through a corn field, and paused at a fence a few yards from the rear of the house. It suddenly dawned on the citizens that they were, according to the *History of Carroll County*, "indifferently armed" to be going up against seasoned guerrillas famous for the firepower of their Navy Colt revolvers. Upon a signal from their leader, however, the citizens swallowed their fear and poured a volley into the entry of the home.

Furniture splintered, and pandemonium momentarily broke loose inside the home as occupants stampeded in every direction. Mrs. Calvert, who was standing near the doorway, was slightly wounded in the breast, and her baby, being held by a bushwhacker nearby, was also struck and slightly injured. Another stray bullet hit Susan Mitchell in the hand. During the confusion, Dugan and Darr made a dash for freedom, and Darr made good his escape. Dugan, though, was less fortunate.

Racing outside, he was shot dead by one of his own neighbors who, in his excitement, mistook the fleeing man for a bushwhacker.

The guerrillas quickly rallied and knocked out the chinking between some of the logs of the house. Using the openings as portholes, they returned the fire of the home guards. The shooting caused some of the citizens' horses to break away, and "the citizens themselves, seeing what a miserable failure their attack had proved, retreated."

The bushwhackers sprang to their saddles and gave chase. One of the citizens, John Kirker, fell from his horse during his escape attempt, and a guerrilla named John Maupin came upon him and shot him. Maupin then leaped from his horse, scalped Kirker, and "with his bowie knife, cut off his head, mutilating the body in a shocking manner." Several other citizens were injured during their escape but none seriously.

During the melee, Caroline Mitchell darted for a neighbor's house. Anderson followed and yelled for her to stop. When she disregarded the command and kept running, he took aim with his revolver and brought her down with a shot through the shoulder.[13] Some of Anderson's own men upbraided him for shooting a woman, but the leader dismissed their objection nonchalantly. "Well," he told them, "it has got to come to that before long anyhow."

At Lawrence, despite the fact that the guerrillas were vitiated with liquor, despite the fact that five Missouri girls had been "murdered" by the Union army just eight days earlier, despite the fact that the "brave and plucky" women of Lawrence, as Quantrill called them, opposed the guerrillas at every turn, the Missourians had strictly obeyed their leader's admonition against molesting women and children. The guerrillas' firm adherence to the interdiction no doubt reinforced their belief that they, not the Union, were the chivalrous protectors of womanhood and family. Only Federal soldiers, they told themselves, would stoop so low as to kill innocent girls.

The elevation of women was at the center of the code by which guerrillas affirmed their moral superiority. Women were pure and good, and it was the role of men to defend, not despoil, them. But now Anderson had crossed even that line and was fast losing his tenuous grip on humanity.

Among his men, scalping had become routine by August of 1864, and horses were killed for sport. At the Mitchell farm, the gang added to its list of atrocities the beheading of a corpse and the deliberate shooting of a woman. As the long summer wore on, Bill Anderson descended deeper and deeper into savagery.

CHAPTER TEN

I Will Hunt You Down Like Wolves

Still in the neighborhood of the Mary Mitchell farm, the guerrillas came to the home of Mary's son, Stephen Mitchell, whose wife Anderson had just shot. They plundered and burned the house and then took a Mr. Latham prisoner and forced him to guide them. They next looted and burned the home of Mrs. John Nance. Passing on, they came to the house of John Hays and robbed it but did not burn it. From the Hays place the bushwhackers struck through the fields to the small community of San Francisco, where they took two men named Henderson and Baker as prisoners and released Latham.

Next they went to the house of Thomas Matthews and took the homeowner and a guest named William Graham captive before resuming their flight. Two companies of militia arrived at the Matthews place just fifteen minutes behind the Anderson gang but had to call off their pursuit because of the gathering darkness. The bushwhackers rode west for another few hours and camped about midnight.

The next morning, Anderson broke camp about daylight and just inside Ray County came upon a man named Russell and his son, who was a Federal officer home on leave. After striking up a conversation with the unsuspecting men, the bushwhackers suddenly shot them down. Afterward, according to the *History of Carroll County*, the guerrillas "jumped from their horses and stripped and robbed them, and rode away with the wailings of the murdered men's family in their ears."[1]

The blue-clad bushwhackers soon met a young man named Oliphant, whom they accosted on the road. "What are you?" Anderson demanded.

"I am a Union man," Oliphant answered.

"Can you kill a bushwhacker?"

"Yes, I can."

"Well, damn you," Anderson swore, "you'll never have a better chance, for we're all bushwhackers."

The guerrillas then began tormenting the young man, dismounted him from the mule he was riding, stripped off his clothes, and whipped him with switches until he was nearly dead. They tied a noose in the middle of the mule's bridle reins and looped it around Oliphant's neck. Then they took off the saddle and tied it to the animal's tail with the intention of frightening it into running and dragging its unfortunate master by the neck. The gentle mule, though, took just a few steps and stopped. The bushwhackers, according to a report of the August 12, 1864, *Carrollton Democrat*, "not being satisfied, again followed it and started it off, determined that the mule should if possible kill the young man." Neither the newspaper account nor the county history makes clear whether the guerrillas accomplished their devilish aim, but apparently not, since the young man must have lived to tell the story.

About 125 militiamen from Carroll and Ray counties chased Anderson throughout the morning. One party got within sight of the guerrillas several times and skirmished with them on one occasion but failed to kill, wound, or capture any of Anderson's small band. The Carroll County contingent soon fell back, gladly turning over the pursuit to their Ray County neighbors. North of Richmond in central Ray, the bushwhackers, having shaken off their pursuers, released unharmed the four men they had taken as captives back in Carroll County.

The guerrillas continued west and hooked up with some of Fletch Taylor's men, including Frank and Jesse James, after Taylor himself was seriously wounded on August 8. During the next couple of days, according to the *Liberty Tribune,* the bushwhackers occupied themselves in Clay County "taking what horses they needed, and all the arms and money they could find." The editor cautioned that the gang, swollen to as many as seventy-five men, was "under the command of that infamous desperado Billy Anderson."[2]

The editor of the *St. Joseph Morning Herald* was even more alarmed by Anderson's appearance in neighboring Clay County than the hometown *Tribune.* "The most heartless, cold-blooded bushwhacking scoundrel that has operated in Missouri since the outbreak of the war," opined the editor in the August 10 issue, "is Bill Anderson. . . . Quantrell, Todd, Thornton, Thrailkill, and others we might name, have written their names high upon the pages of infamy, but Bill Anderson overtops them all in crime."

The editor advanced his argument by recounting the grisly report of a Union man recently taken prisoner and brutally killed by Anderson. According to the *Morning Herald,* the man had his nose and ears cut off while still alive, before being shot to death and riddled with bullets.

The outraged editor had no way of knowing that the worst was yet to come.

Leaving Camp Branch on August 10, Anderson's band started east through Clay County and on the evening of the 12th ambushed a twenty-five-man militia company at Fredericksburg in western Ray County. After a desperate fight, the guerrillas dispersed the Yankees, leaving the commander, Capt. Patten Colley, and four of his men dead on the ground. Anderson himself reportedly fired the shot that killed Colley.[3] Telegraph wires buzzed with news of the attack, and Federal units from all around hurried to the chase.

General Fisk sent orders to Colonel Shanklin at Chillicothe to let all his fighting men "be exclusively an Anderson extermination party."[4] In another communication the general added, "Anderson is the worst of all, and he must be killed, or he will cause the death of every Union man he can find."[5] More and more during the summer of 1864, the Federal effort in northern Missouri centered around one task—stopping Bill Anderson.

After routing the militia at Fredericksburg, Anderson struck northeast and the next morning was on the Knoxville road in the northern part of Ray County. Here the guerrillas intercepted two soldiers, named Daniel Vanzant and Samuel Forson, who were on their way from Richmond to Knoxville with military dispatches. They shot Forson, sliced his throat from ear to ear, and scalped him. They put a bullet in Vanzant's head and trampled his body beneath their horses. A little farther on, the bushwhackers killed a citizen militiaman named James Maupin who was driving along the road in his wagon. They also stole horses, burned a house, and committed a number of other minor depredations in the area.

Around noon, the guerrillas angled southeast, crossed into southern Carroll County during the early evening, and arrived at Hill's Landing on the Missouri River about ten o'clock at night. Here they killed a militiaman named James Warren, who was awaiting a steamer to take him back to his command. The bushwhackers then camped for the night not far away, having traveled forty miles that day. Their much-needed rest, though, didn't last long. Several hundred Yankees soldiers were bearing down on them.

The next morning, August 14, Anderson moved off to the east at a leisurely pace, seemingly inviting an attack from the garrison at Carrollton, but the commander there was indisposed to launch such an assault without reinforcements. Militiamen throughout the county were called in, but many of them apparently were even more disinclined to fight Anderson than their commander. One such reluctant soldier, a man named Kelly, was accosted on his way to the rendezvous.

"Where are you going, Kelly?" his inquisitor asked.

"A-huntin'."

"Hunting? Hunting what?"

"Something I don't want to find."

"What is that?"

"Bill Anderson, the murderin' blaggard, and may the devil fly away with him."

The anonymous author of the *Carroll County History* surmised that "there were many others besides Kelly who hunted Bill Anderson with the fervent hope that they might not find him."[6] Nevertheless, a combined force of militia from Carroll and Ray counties numbering at least 150 men set off in pursuit shortly before noon.

In the meantime, Anderson was busy killing and marauding near the crossing of Sambo Slough southeast of Carrollton. His gang met an old man named Chapman and shot him several times. They plundered several houses in the neighborhood, including one belonging to a Union cavalryman. The bushwhackers stole some of the man's belongings and told his wife that her husband was a "goddamned abolitionist, and ought to be killed."[7] They also took a man named Fox prisoner before moving off to some timber about a mile to the east.

The militia came upon and charged the guerrillas while they were still camped in the brush. The bushwhackers killed their prisoner during the first exchange of fire, then sprang to their saddles and countercharged, driving the Federals back.

Apparently the militia force contained a large number of dubious warriors like Kelly. Only about fifty men had obeyed the commander's order to charge, while at least double that number lingered back in relative safety. Regrouping, however, the militia mounted a second charge that forced the guerrillas to retreat.

The exact numbers of killed and wounded during the fierce thirty-minute battle vary with the source, but at least five Union soldiers and one bushwhacker were known dead. Among the guerrillas injured were Anderson himself, Arch Clement, Peyton Long, Frank James, and Jesse James. Maj. John Grimes, commander of Enrolled Missouri Militia at Richmond, claimed in an August 18 report, "There is every reason to believe that their leader, Anderson, is either dead or mortally wounded." This proved to be a bit of wishful thinking, however, as Jesse James was the only guerrilla seriously hurt.[8] He was carried to the home of a Confederate sympathizer, where he was nursed back to health. Several of the other wounded Rebels also found refuge among Southern sympathizers in the county.

Moving off to the east, Anderson had time to tend to his wounded before the Yankees organized a pursuit. By the time the militia reached the Rock Ford at Grand River, the guerrillas had already crossed, and the pursuit was called off. Anderson passed leisurely through Chariton and Howard counties unmolested and rendezvoused with the guerrilla band of Clifton Holtzclaw in the Perche Hills of western Boone around August 19.

Following Anderson's latest outrages in Carroll County, the Union once again "made it hot" for Confederate sympathizers in the area.[9] Families of bushwhackers were exiled, fines were levied on citizens who were considered disloyal, and those even suspected of aiding the guerrillas were maltreated.

On August 20 near Rocheport, Anderson's gang skirmished with a company of the Seventeenth Illinois Cavalry and wounded one man severely before scattering into the brush. The commanding officer at Glasgow complained that the guerrillas had been able to approach the Union force by using signals and passwords stolen from the Federals.

Throughout the next week, Anderson and his men lurked in their hideouts in the Perche Hills, emerging during the day only long enough to attack a passing steamer on the Missouri River or harass some other Union target. On August 23, twelve miles below Glasgow the steamboat *Omaha*, bound for Leavenworth with government supplies, was attacked, perhaps by some of Anderson's roving band.[10] One passenger was seriously wounded, and the anxious captain refused to continue his journey beyond Glasgow until a gunboat could be sent to escort him.

At night, though, the guerrillas retreated to their hideouts around Rocheport, where they reportedly gathered for nightly "carnivals" to celebrate their successes over the Yankees.[11]

Union officers, meanwhile, bragged of their own accomplishments, bolstering their claims with a generous count of enemy casualties. Dispatches received by General Fisk from his subordinates on August 24 alone reported forty-one guerrillas "mustered out" in the lower counties of the general's district.[12] Furthermore, Fisk pledged that he and his men were "doing all we can ... to exterminate the murdering fiends."[13] About the same time, Fisk urged his junior officers that the people around Rocheport "be made to understand that there is something besides Bill Anderson power in North Missouri."[14]

To that end, Union commanders stepped up their vigilance in the area. Brig. Gen J. B. Douglass, stationed now at Fayette, sent out a party under Maj. Reeves Leonard that skirmished with Anderson's men three separate times near Rocheport on August 27, putting the bushwhackers to rout and killing three or four with only one Federal soldier wounded. Leonard, however, soon came under attack for not annihilating Anderson, the implication being that he and his men were less than zealous in carrying out their task.

On August 28, a forty-four-man scout of the Fourth Missouri Cavalry at Boonville crossed the river into Howard County and rode east with the express purpose of hunting down Anderson. Led by Capt. Joseph Parke, the squad discovered two bushwhackers about four miles north of Rocheport and fired upon them. One was wounded, and both horses were captured, but the two men escaped to the woods on foot.

About a mile farther down the road, Anderson and Holtzclaw waited in ambush. They had been informed of the Union scouting party on their trail and had formed their men behind the brow of a hill where the road narrowed to a lane passing through some woods. When the Federals reached the entrance to the lane, the band of seventy-five to a hundred screaming guerrillas suddenly charged over the hill with guns blazing. Parke formed his men in a line, but the line broke almost immediately and the Yankees scattered in confusion, leaving seven soldiers dead on the ground.

The bushwhackers pounced on the corpses with savage vengeance. They scalped four, slit the throats of three, and hung one of the scalped men from a nearby tree. They also killed six Union horses and wounded several others.

Parke reassembled his scattered troops, enlisted the support of Major Leonard, and returned to the field of battle to drive off the bushwhackers. The September 2, 1864, *Columbia Missouri Statesman* described in further detail the gory scene he found:

> The Federal dead were scalped and otherwise lacerated by these demons. ... From the heads of some almost the entire scalp was skinned off; from others only a small piece was cut out about the size of a silver dollar. From the foreheads of others small strips of skin were cut out; all to be carried as trophies by these incarnate fiends.

Parke gathered up his dead and returned the seven bodies to Boonville for burial. A dead Union soldier found in the brush in the vicinity of the battle two days later brought the number killed to eight. Guerrilla losses were estimated at two men killed, although the exact number is uncertain since the bushwhackers were able to carry off their dead and wounded. Hamp Watts, a member of Anderson's band who recalled his war experiences in a 1913 booklet entitled *The Babe of the Company*, said no guerrillas were killed in the skirmish.

Anderson lingered in the area around Rocheport, where the rowdy bushwhackers robbed Union stores and citizens and, in the words of historian Richard Brownlee, "drank the saloons dry."[15] On the evening of August 30, from a bluff just above the town, they fired into the steam tug *Buffington,* which had come up the river from the state prison at Jefferson City. The captain of the boat, Thomas Waterman, was killed and a clerk wounded. When the boat came to shore, the guerrillas commandeered the craft and had a grand time shouting and churning up and down the river, "outrageously pleased at having a private navy."[16]

Union officials reacted to the murder of Waterman by assessing a fine of $10,000 on the traitorous citizens of Rocheport for having fed and supported the bushwhackers during the prior six weeks. The money was to go to Waterman's family.

Anderson and his wild crew continued to carouse around Rocheport. On September 5 they fired into the steamboat *Yellowstone* as she passed on her way downriver. The guerrillas followed the boat for some distance, blasting away at the fleeing vessel. When the *Mars* appeared upriver at about the same time, the gang redirected its fusillade at the new target and demanded the steamer's surrender as they trailed her back to Rocheport. The *Mars* stopped in the channel of the river, and two impulsive bushwhackers named Emory and Rucker, misinterpreting the act as a signal of compliance, hopped in a skiff and rowed out into the river toward the steamboat. Guards on the *Mars* fired at the foolish pair, mortally wounding Rucker, and the craft retreated safely downriver. Anderson's repeated attacks on passing vessels, however, had brought traffic on the Missouri River to a virtual standstill.[17]

With the Perche Hills still serving as a sanctuary, Anderson's men marauded throughout Howard County in small bands during the middle of September, robbing stages and halting the mail between the military posts of Fayette, Franklin, and Renick. On the 12th, Anderson and some of his men robbed a blacksmith shop in Rocheport of all the horseshoes and horseshoe nails they could find and also broke into a saddlery shop and stole leather.[18]

The same day, a Union patrol near Franklin surprised a separate Anderson party that had stopped at the home of a Southern sympathizer for the noon meal. Three guerrillas were killed as they fled, while three others reached the brush safely. Another, named Lee McMurtry, managed to escape detection, according to Watts, by hiding his pistols and convincing the Federals that he was a civilian member of the household. (The ruse was later discovered, and a young lady who had helped McMurtry was banished from the district.) The bridle of one of the bushwhackers' horses captured at the house was adorned with human scalps. The Union patrol killed two more guerrillas in the vicinity the same day.[19]

On September 23 a band of seven bushwhackers were on the road between Fayette and Rocheport, having been commissioned by Anderson, according to Watts, "to collect from noncombatants a 'Contributive Tax' for the support and maintenance of his company."[20] In plain language, the guerrillas were stealing from civilians, although Watts claims the so-called levy was strictly voluntary.

A rain came up, and the small band sought refuge at the farm of a Mrs. Turner. While the guerrillas were holed up in the barn, a scouting party of Major Leonard's Ninth Cavalry Missouri State Militia on its way from Fayette to Rocheport happened along and were directed to the barn by a Negro man working in a nearby field.

The road was hidden from the bushwhackers' view by an orchard and a corn field, and the Federals got to within a short distance of the barn before the guerrillas spotted them. The soldiers charged, killing six of the seven bushwhackers as they fled. The Federals captured all seven of the guerrillas' horses, took thirty revolvers off the dead men, and scalped the corpses.

Other members of Anderson's gang came along shortly afterward and, beholding the fate of their comrades, vowed quick revenge. One of the soldiers who was with the Federal scouting party later allowed that Anderson and his men "got their revenge, but not on our regiment."[21]

An indirect sort of revenge came sooner than even Anderson's men could have imagined. Later the same day, George Todd and John Thrailkill, at the head of over a hundred guerrillas and fresh from a raid through Chariton County, swept down on a Union wagon train about ten miles north of Rocheport in Boone County, killing twelve soldiers of the escort and three Negro teamsters.[22] Todd then turned back into Howard County and went into camp south of Fayette late that night.

Official Union reports and newspaper accounts immediately suggested that Anderson had led the raid on the wagon train, but he was in Howard County at the time. By the fall of 1864 Anderson had become as ubiquitous as Quantrill. The latter, an omnipresent devil in the minds of loyal citizens and Union officials, was reportedly spotted far and wide all summer long despite hiding out in Howard County with Kate Clarke. Now a far-flung frenzy of violence during the past three months had earned "the notorious Bill Anderson" a similar reputation for unbounded evil among apprehensive Union observers.[23]

On the evening of September 23, about the time the raid on the wagon train took place, Anderson was still busy collecting his gang at the Turner farm, the same location where his six men had been killed and scalped earlier that day. Anderson was furious. The Federals had given him a dose of his own medicine that left him foaming at the mouth. The next Yankees who got into his clutches would pay a dear price.

Anderson's band camped that night on Bonne Femme Creek near the Turner farm. The next morning at daybreak, they mounted up and rode into Todd and Thrailkill's camp, not far away. Frank Smith, one of Todd's men, was aghast to see human scalps dangling from the bridles of some of the arriving horses.

Quantrill momentarily put aside his differences with his old lieutenants and came out of hiding to join the rendezvous as well. The truce, however, didn't last long.

Still stinging from the Federal outrage on his men the previous day, Anderson proposed attacking Fayette, where Major Leonard's Ninth Cavalry was headquartered. Quantrill, who had had some edifying experiences in attacking brick buildings, argued against the assault and refused to accept command of the assembled force. He said the place was too heavily fortified and that too many guerrillas would be killed.

Todd, though, agreed with Anderson, and the two leaders argued with their old chieftain. They made derogatory remarks about Quantrill's sand being gone and about the "military discipline of Kate Clarke."[24] Anderson and Todd finally said they were going to Fayette regardless and that Quantrill could either come along or go back to the woods with the rest of the cowards. Quantrill reluctantly agreed to go along. Anderson took charge of the mission and volunteered his band to lead the assault.

The guerrillas marched north toward Fayette and about ten-thirty that morning reached the outskirts, where they paused to form in a column. The command then proceeded into town with Anderson leading the advance. Garbed in Federal blue, the bushwhackers created little alarm at first and might have been able to surprise and overwhelm the garrison had not a guerrilla with an itchy trigger finger opened fire on a Negro who was standing on the sidewalk, wearing a blue uniform. At this warning, civilians rushed for safety, and the garrison of about fifty soldiers took up their strongholds in the brick courthouse and in a blockhouse fortified with heavy railroad ties.

The bushwhackers threw their horses into a gallop. Todd's men dashed onto the courthouse square, while Anderson and his crew raced to the blockhouse located on a small hill at the north edge of town.

Here, in the words of Hamp Watts, Anderson's "wild, wanton, stupid assault on the log house" began. "Not one of the enemy could be seen," according to Watts, "but the muzzles of muskets protruded from every port hole, belching fire and lead at the charging guerrillas. Horses went down as grain before the reaper." [25]

Having been repelled at the courthouse, Todd joined Anderson as the latter retreated from the blockhouse with several of his men lying wounded or dead on the open field. Seeing what a debacle the first charge had been, Todd grew furious and led a charge of his own. His wild assault proved just as futile as the first, and again several of the screaming guerrillas toppled from their saddles as they blasted away at unseen targets.

Still incensed, Todd ordered yet another charge. The bushwhackers, though, after witnessing the dismal outcome of the first two attempts, had shed their enthusiasm for the enterprise, and the third charge was reduced to "a mere feint." [26]

Anderson and Todd had finally learned what Quantrill had tried to tell them about the senselessness of assaulting fortified buildings, but the realization didn't stop Todd from blaming his old chieftain for the failure of the attack. Seeing the futility of the assault, Quantrill had retired to the edge of town early on, and now Todd sought to kill him for his discretion. Only the pleading of his men and their refusal to participate in the murder managed to dissuade the fuming Todd.

The guerrillas stole carriages in which to haul their wounded as they retreated along the north road. They left five dead on the ground, and several who were loaded into the wagons were either already dead or injured so severely that they later died. Miraculously enough, however, both Anderson and Todd came through the assaults unscathed, despite having ridden at the head of the reckless charges.

Only two Federals were killed and two wounded. One of the dead, a sentry named Benton who had the misfortune of being caught in an open field at the edge of town, was found scalped, and the trophy of the heinous work was nailed to a tree. Beside the scalp someone had scrawled and pinned an inscription that read, "This is the way we do business."[27]

Years later, Hamp Watts would blame the miserable result of the guerrilla attack on "Bill Anderson's reckless foolhardiness."[28] Frank James, too, had bleak memories of Fayette. He called it "the worst fight I ever had" and said he was more frightened during the ill-fated assault on the blockhouse than at any other time during the war.[29]

The bushwhackers left their wounded with sympathetic civilians along the road north of Fayette and camped that night east of Roanoke on the farm of Judge John Viley. The next morning they continued north and reached the Huntsville area about noon. Anderson sent a civilian messenger into town, demanding its surrender in the name of "the Southern Confederacy."[30] Lieutenant Colonel Denny replied that if the guerrillas wanted the place they would have to come in and take it. Anderson was ready to oblige, but Todd, who had gotten his fill at Fayette of assailing brick buildings, could not be persuaded this time.[31]

The guerrillas moved off to the southeast toward Renick, tearing down telegraph wires all along the way. Again Union patrols were in hot pursuit, eager to carry out General Fisk's order to "Find and kill the devils."[32] The scouting parties managed to catch up to a few stragglers, and Fisk boasted that these laggards were "summarily mustered out."[33]

The guerrillas camped that night near Renick and on the morning of September 26 headed northeast into Monroe County. They passed Middle Grove around noon and later in the day threatened the county seat at Paris. Upon learning that the town contained a sizeable militia force, they retreated south into Audrain County. That evening, Maj. A. V. E. Johnston mounted up about 150 soldiers of the Thirty-ninth Missouri Infantry Volunteers and left Paris in pursuit of the bushwhackers.

The guerrillas stopped to rest in a timbered area on Young's Creek. While there, Anderson's pickets were mistaken for Federals and fired upon by some of G. W. Bryson's bushwhackers, who were under the overall command of Confederate recruiting officer Caleb Perkins. Realizing their mistake, Bryson's men sent a lieutenant to explain the error and to suggest that the two parties join forces. Anderson grew irate and gave the messenger a tongue-lashing. "Your men are either damned fools or worse," he said, "or you would not have fired at us. I don't want anything to do with you or any other of Perkins' men."[34]

The march continued south along the creek. Around dark the guerrillas crossed the North Missouri Railroad in Boone County and shortly afterward went into camp at the farm of M. G. Singleton, a former Confederate officer. Close to three hundred guerrillas sat around the fires that night, recalling recent escapades of the war and boasting of General Price's great invasion of Missouri that promised to take back the state for the Confederacy. Meanwhile, the quiet little hamlet of Centralia, two and a half miles northwest of the farm, slept unaware.

CHAPTER ELEVEN

Every Federal Soldier Shall Die Like a Dog

The next morning about ten o'clock, Anderson and his band of seventy-five men scouted out to see if any Federals were on the trail of the bushwhackers. Discovering none, they rode into Centralia, a way station on the North Missouri Railroad, to try to get news of Price's movements.

A few of Bryson's guerrillas were in town to solicit the services of Dr. A. F. Sneed for their captain, who had been wounded the day before in a skirmish with Johnston's troops. These men informed Anderson of the major's presence in the area but assured him the Federal command was poorly armed and mounted.

The guerrillas quickly took over the village, which, in addition to the depot, consisted of just four businesses and about a dozen homes. Some of the gang broke into houses, demanding breakfast, while others robbed the town's two stores. Anderson himself rode straight to the Eldorado House, one of two hotels in the village, and struck up a pleasant conversation with the landlord, J. J. Collier.

At the stores, the bushwhackers stole virtually every article they could get their hands on, including many for which they had no use—calico cloth, women's shoes, and even baby slippers. At the depot, though, they found some goods boxed up in the freight house awaiting transportation to Columbia that were more along their line. The guerrillas broke open and appropriated three or four cases of boots and also discovered a large barrel of whiskey. Within five seconds, according to the *History of Boone County,* "the head was broken in and 'anti-prohibition' flowed down the throats of the guerrillas like water after a long and sultry ride."[1]

News of the whiskey spread quickly, and soon nearly all the bushwhackers, including Anderson himself, had tasted it. The county history suggested that "experts of the border alone can accomplish a convivial feat of that character." Because the barrel was too heavy to carry, the question occurred as to how the guerrillas could transport some of the whiskey back to camp so their comrades "might share with them its exhilarating influence, and it was soon decided that some of the new boots should serve the office of demijohns."

At eleven o'clock the stage from Columbia rolled into town and was quickly swarmed by bushwhackers. A few dismounted and jerked open the doors, demanding to know if there were any Federal soldiers inside. None of the passengers were soldiers, but several were prominent Union men on their way to Mexico, Missouri, as delegates to the Democratic Congressional Convention. Two, Boone County Sheriff James H. Waugh and Congressman James S. Rollins, were in particular danger because of the offices they held.

With a wave of their guns, the guerrillas ordered the men off the stage. As the passengers disembarked, they were met with cocked revolvers pressed against their chests. "Hand out your pocketbooks," the gang demanded, "all of you."

"We are Southern men and Confederate sympathizers," complained one man artfully. "You ought not to rob us."

"What do we care? Hell's full of all such Southern men. Why ain't you out fightin'?"

The bushwhackers fired questions at the passengers as they relieved the men of their money. Taking a cue from their fellow passenger, Rollins and Waugh fabricated stories in hopes of escaping a fate worse than being robbed. Rollins said his name was Johnson and that he was "a minister of the Methodist Church, South." Sheriff Waugh claimed his name was Smith. Another man bragged of having been arrested by the Union army.

After all the pocketbooks and other valuables had been seized, the bushwhackers prepared to search the men. Rollins and Waugh knew a special moment of fear, for they both carried papers revealing their true identities and Rollins had his name stamped in indelible ink on his clothing. Just as the search began, though, a cry went up that diverted the attention of the robbers. "The train! The train! Yonder comes the train!" The guerrillas raced toward the depot 250 yards away in search of bigger spoils.

The train, bound from St. Louis on its regular run to St. Joseph, consisted of three passenger coaches, an express coach, and a baggage car. On board were twenty-three discharged and furloughed Federal soldiers on their way home from Sherman's army and 125 other passengers—men, women, and children.

Engineer James Clark spotted the mob of bushwhackers mounted on horseback near the depot when the train was still two miles east of Centralia, but since many were clad in blue, he assumed them to be Federal troops. "It was not unusual in those days," Clark explained in 1896, "to find them [state troops] any place and at most any station along the line."[2]

As the train slowed about a mile from the depot, though, the passengers and crew saw some of the bushwhackers lined up along the south side of the track opposite the station platform, and suspicions grew. One of the soldiers, a member of the First Iowa Cavalry, cried out, "Those men are guerrillas!"

Then, as the train drew near the station, Clark saw Anderson's men piling ties and other obstructions on the track, and he cautioned his fireman "to look out for himself."[3] Fear of colliding with a gravel train that had left Mexico close behind the passenger train may have deterred the engineer from trying to stop and reverse course. Instead, he determined to go straight ahead and break through the blockade if the obstructions did not derail the train. "I pulled the throttle wide open and dropped on the deck," recalled Clark.

Anderson's men, however, opened fire with "a perfect shower of bullets," and the brakemen, according to Clark, sought refuge in the coaches and "left the brakes all set tight, which brought the train to a stop in front of the depot." The throttle was still wide open, causing the wheels of the engine to spin on the tracks, and the guerrillas kept up their fusillade as long as the wheels kept spinning.[4] "So I raised up and shut off the throttle," Clark said, "and then dropped on the deck again."

Immediately several guerrillas sprang into the cab with cocked revolvers and relieved the engineer and his fireman of their money and other valuables. The fireman, who'd been winged during the hail of gunfire and was bleeding lavishly from the superficial wound, cried out, "For God's sake, don't kill us."[5]

"We don't want to harm any of you men," one of the bushwhackers assured him, "but consider yourselves prisoners and obey orders."

The fireman, Jack Kirkby, was ordered off the train and enjoined by a guerrilla to hold some of the bushwhackers' horses. "If you let my horses get away," the raider warned, "I will blow your damned head off."[6]

Clark was also "called into service" and ordered to take down the large Union flags he had displayed on either side of the train's headlight. Half a dozen bushwhackers crowded around the engineer with leveled revolvers to ensure speedy compliance with the decree.

A squad of bushwhackers led by Little Archie Clement thronged into the passenger cars, demanding that the soldiers give themselves up. "Surrender!" the guerrillas cried. "Surrender! You are prisoners of war."

The soldiers, who had but two revolvers among them, quietly submitted. A few wryly observed that they had no choice but to surrender since they were unarmed. The twenty-three soldiers were cursed and robbed, then herded outside with kicks and prods and formed in a group. Many were stripped of their uniforms so that guerrillas who lacked Federal outfits could don the blue.

Driven outside with the soldiers was a German man from St. Louis, who had the misfortune to be wearing a blue shirt and a soldier's cap. He tried to remonstrate but couldn't speak English fluently enough to make himself understood. Had he been able to articulate his predicament, he still might not have saved himself, since the guerrillas hated "Dutchmen" categorically.

The bushwhackers also ordered the passengers off the train and robbed them. Men, women, and even children were divested of pocketbooks, knives, watches, jewelry, clothing, trinkets, and other items as they disembarked. Women and children sobbed or moaned as the guerrillas shouted threats and flourished their revolvers. Occasionally an impatient bushwhacker fired a shot overhead to encourage a reluctant victim to fork over.

A young man who was traveling to St. Joseph with his mother was robbed and told that, if he had any more money, he had better deliver it, because he would be searched later on. As he handed over his pocketbook, he assured the guerrillas that he had nothing else, even though he had secreted a hundred dollars in greenbacks in his boot. Later, he admitted the deception but was gunned down, nonetheless, for having lied in the first place.[7]

After the passengers were forced off the train and robbed, according to the *History of Boone County*, "they huddled in groups about the grounds adjoining, clinging to each other, and not daring to leave without permission."

A detail led by Anderson himself entered the express car, compelled the express messenger to hand over his keys, and stole $3,000 from the safe. Suddenly whoops of celebration came from the adjoining baggage car, and Anderson hurried to see what the commotion was.

Peyton Long and others had found a valise containing a reported $10,000.[8] "Good God! Here's thousands of greenbacks!" cried the jubilant bushwhackers. They crammed their pockets with currency, then ransacked the baggage car in search of more loot. The guerrillas broke open every trunk and piece of luggage they could find, spilling the contents onto the floor.

When he stepped back outside, Anderson ordered that the soldiers be marched to the south side of the railroad tracks and formed in a line. Then he mounted his horse and followed. Arch Clement and his villainous squad had the trembling Federals under guard as Anderson rode up. "What are you going to do with them fellows?" Clement asked.

A twisted grin crossed Anderson's face. "*Parole* them, of course."

"I thought so," Clement said with a laugh. "You might pick out two or three, though, and exchange them for Cave, if you can." Cave Wyatt, a sergeant in Anderson's company, had been wounded during the August fight in Carroll County and had fallen into Union hands.

"Oh, one will be enough for that," Anderson judged. "Arch, you take charge of the firing party, and, when I give the word, pour hell into them."

Anderson turned to face the line of soldiers. Dressed in black pants tucked into high cavalry boots, a Federal overcoat, and a slouch hat with the brim pinned back at an angle, Anderson drew himself up and struck a rakish pose. Then he began to harangue the soldiers in a loud voice:

> You Federals have just killed six of my soldiers, scalped them, and left them on the prairie. I am too honorable a man to permit any man to be scalped, but I will show you that I can kill men with as much rapidity and skill as anybody. From this time forward I ask no quarter, and give none. Every Federal soldier on whom I put my fingers shall die like a dog. If I get into your clutches I expect death. You are all to be killed and sent to hell. That is the way every damned soldier shall be served who falls into my hands.[9]

Some of the soldiers protested that they had come straight from Sherman's army and had no part whatsoever in killing or scalping any of Anderson's men.

"I treat you all as one," Anderson snapped. "You are Federals, and Federals scalped my men, and carry their scalps at their saddle-bows."[10]

Although Major Leonard's command had, in fact, scalped Anderson's men four days earlier, the guerrilla chief's speech was still a remarkable feat of psychological contortionism, as he had managed to deny the very behavior for which he was infamous, assigning it exclusively to the enemy.

Anderson then adopted a more affable tone as he continued to address the soldiers. "Boys, have you a sergeant in your ranks?"

There were several, but they were afraid Anderson meant to single them out for special torture. No one answered.

"I say," he repeated in a louder voice, "is there a sergeant in the line? If there be one, let him step aside."

Reluctantly, Sgt. Thomas Goodman stepped forward, and Anderson detailed two men to escort the prisoner to safety near a small stable. Anderson then turned and gave the signal Arch Clement had been waiting for. The murderous crew of about twenty-five guerrillas "poured hell" into the captives from twenty paces away.

Despite being expert pistol shots, many of the drunken bushwhackers missed their aim, and only about half the prisoners dropped at the first volley. The remainder stumbled about screaming, groaning, and clutching their wounds as Clement's ruthless squad rained lead at them,

From his position of safety, Goodman turned when he heard the sounds of gunfire and the cries and moans of his fellow soldiers. "The line had disappeared," he wrote in a pamphlet published in 1868. "Many of my late comrades lay dead upon the ground, others were groaning in the agony of their wounds, and yet others, wounded and suffering, were making a last struggle for existence."[11]

One of the latter was a giant of a man named Sgt. Valentine Peters. Shot five times through the body and dressed just in his drawers and undershirt, he suddenly charged the guerrilla line, knocking bushwhackers left and right. He broke through and managed to reach the depot, where he hid under the platform, which was several feet above the ground. The guerrillas, though, had set the depot on fire, and the heat forced Peters from his refuge. He was dragged out and shot through the head.

Others of the wounded, according to the *History of Boone County,*

> wandered about, stunned and bleeding, and in their agony staggered against the very muzzles of the revolvers of the guerrillas. One or two started for the railroad, and fell dead within a few feet of it. Some cried, "O, God, have mercy!" but the most of them merely groaned and moaned in the most agonizing manner. The poor German whined pitifully as he expired.... One man lay flat on his back, with his hands clinched tightly in the short grass. Another lay with one bullet-hole over his eye, another in his face, a third in his breast. He was unconscious, his eyes were closed, he did not moan, but, with a sort of spasmodic motion, he dragged his right heel on the ground, back and forth, back and forth. "He's marking time," said Arch Clement, jocosely.

Anderson's men tramped among the lifeless bodies, stabbing the prostrate forms with sabers, pounding them with the butts of their revolvers, or kicking them with heavy boots. Any soldier who showed signs of life was put out of his misery with a bullet through the head. According to Goodman, "The guerrillas, with horrid oaths and wild fierce looks, gloated over the bodies of the slain, or spurned them from their path with brutal violence."[12]

The passengers and citizens who had witnessed the carnage were mute with horror. Many of the women sobbed or whispered silent prayers while some of the men recoiled in disgust from the gruesome scene and ambled off in a daze, as far away as they could get. A few, though, got up nerve to approach Anderson. "May we go on to Sturgeon?" one of them asked.

"Go on to hell, for all I care," Anderson growled.

He made sure, though, that, wherever they planned to go,

they weren't going to get there by rail. Compelling the crew and bystanders to help, the bushwhackers set the coaches and baggage car of the train ablaze. Thomas S. Sneed, proprietor of Sneed's Hotel in Centralia, hurried through the passenger coaches, checking for stragglers who might still be aboard. In one he found a woman and three children huddled together with ashen faces, and he coaxed the trembling group to safety as the flames licked higher.

On a side rail sat nine boxcars, which the guerrillas set on fire, too, meaning to send the depot and surrounding cars up in one giant conflagration. However, the approach of the gravel train, spotted in the distance, prompted a change of plans.

The bushwhackers ordered Engineer Clark to climb into the cab, start the train forward, and then jump clear of it. Clark explained that he would have to back the engine up first so they could remove the obstructions. As soon as that task was accomplished, the guerrillas waved their pistols at the engineer and yelled for him to "turn the engine loose" and "give her hell." [13] Clark set the train in motion and then leaped from the blazing juggernaut.

He had the daring and foresight, though, to put on both of his pumps when he fired up the engine, and the train ran just a short distance toward Sturgeon before the boiler filled with water and the steam died. The train was found later that day about three miles west of Centralia.

The bushwhackers rode out to meet the approaching gravel train while it was still a half-mile away. They swarmed around it, demanding its surrender, and finally brought it to a stop fifty yards short of the depot by tossing one of the dead soldiers across the track. The crew halted rather than run over the corpse, but then the bushwhackers told the engineer to pull the train on up to the platform. When he asked them to remove the body, they refused and ordered him at gunpoint to run over it. He did, and the body derailed the train near the depot. The guerrillas robbed the crew, ordered them to march back toward Mexico, and set the train on fire.

Anderson and his men loaded up their loot and prepared to

Monument on the town square in Centralia to the victims of the Centralia massacre and the battle that followed.

leave. All of them had plunder of some sort bulging from their pockets or strapped behind them in bundles, and many had boots full of whiskey tied together and harnessed across their horses' necks. Sergeant Goodman was mounted on a mule with a guard on either side as the triumphant bushwhackers marched out of town in two columns, whooping and shouting. "The maimed bodies of the Union boys," recalled Goodman, "lay where they had fallen, and here and there wandering listlessly among the slain" were a few civilians.[14]

The bushwhackers rode back to camp southeast of town. After unsaddling and picketing their horses, many dropped to the ground in a whiskey stupor.

CHAPTER TWELVE

I Grew Sick of Killing Them

At midafternoon, Major Johnston, who had been trailing Todd and Anderson all day, came to the place east of Centralia where the guerrillas had crossed the railroad the evening before. The town was in plain view, and when the major saw the smoke from the smoldering depot banked in the sky, he decided to investigate.

The Thirty-ninth Missouri, which had been in service only two weeks, rode into town, according to the *History of Boone County,* mounted on animals "'pressed' from certain 'disloyal' citizens of Monroe, Shelby and Marion Counties..., most of them being old brood-mares and plow-horses, with some indifferent mules."[1] In addition, the soldiers were armed just with muzzle-loading Enfield rifles equipped with bayonets.

As Johnston surveyed the blackened ruins of the depot and the horrid spectacle of slaughtered comrades strewn about the ground, he vowed quick revenge. He knew that the sickening scene was the work of the guerrillas he had been following, but he questioned citizens to learn specific details. They told him that the number who had visited Centralia that morning was no more than 80, but Dr. A. F. Sneed, who had been summoned to treat the guerrilla Bryson and had received some intelligence from that source, cautioned that the total number of bushwhackers in camp southeast of town was nearer 400. The major believed this count to be greatly exaggerated. His own estimate placed the number at no more than 150.

He and Dr. Sneed climbed to the attic of Mr. Thomas Sneed's hotel and looked out the window over the prairie in the direction of the guerrilla camp. They saw a squad of about fifteen men ride out of some timber a mile away. "There they are now!" cried Major Johnston.

As he hurried downstairs, Dr. Sneed followed, demanding to know if the major intended to attack the guerrillas.

"I do!" Johnston declared.

Sneed tried to talk him out of the plan. "They largely outnumber you, and they are much better armed and mounted, having four good revolvers each and splendid horses." He neglected to add that some of the bushwhackers also carried Sharps carbines.

Determined to fight the guerrillas at all costs, Major Johnson lent a fancifully optimistic interpretation to Dr. Sneed's warning. "They may have the advantage of me in numbers but I will have the advantage of them in arms. My guns are of long range and I can fight them successfully from a distance."

Calling his command together, he ordered thirty-five soldiers and two teamsters to stay in Centralia under Capt. Adam Theis and Lt. John E. Stafford. The rest of the command, now numbering no more than 120 men, rode southeast out of town toward the stand of timber where Johnston had spotted the small squad of guerrillas.

* * * * *

When Todd learned what had happened in Centralia that morning, he censured Anderson for the atrocity, and the two men argued briefly. Anderson was about ready to take his band and leave camp when some of Thrailkill's men, who had been acting as pickets, rode in with news that a Federal force of 150 men was at Centralia. At the prospect of battle, Todd and Anderson quickly set aside their differences.

Anderson correctly surmised that the Federal force was the

command Bryson's men had told him about that morning. "They have only old muskets and no revolvers," he said to Todd. "It will be only fun to clean them up."

Todd sent out a party under Dave Pool to check on the movements of the Yankees and to draw them toward the guerrilla camp.[2] This was the squad Johnston had spied emerging from the stand of timber a mile outside town, and now Pool was trolling the unsuspecting Federals in.

Meanwhile, the main body of guerrillas tore down the fence separating their camp from a neighboring farm and entered a fallow field to the west. Todd formed his band along a branch to the south of the field while Thrailkill occupied a similar position along a slough to the north. Anderson, with plans to lead the charge, took the center and assembled his men in a battle line facing west.

Pool waited until Johnston's advance was within two hundred yards, then retreated southward at a leisurely pace. Assured that he was being followed, he galloped away to join his comrades and disappeared over the top of a hill.

When Johnston reached the crest, Anderson's band of about seventy-five men faced him from the crown of a second small hill half a mile away. The rest of the guerrillas were hidden along the branches that bordered the field. The major dismounted his men and advanced ninety of them about a hundred yards. The remaining one-fourth stayed behind to hold the horses, as was common among mounted infantry when fighting on foot.

When John Koger, one of the guerrillas, saw the Yankees dismount, he couldn't believe his eyes. "Why the fools are going to fight us on foot! God help 'em."[3]

Some of Anderson's men dismounted to tighten their cinches, then swung back to their saddles. Anderson rode along the line, giving last-minute instructions. "Boys, when we charge, break through the line and keep straight on for the horses. Keep straight on for the horses!"

A final time he surveyed the dismounted Federal soldiers, their muskets and bayonets glistening under the blue autumn sky. "Not a damned revolver in the crowd!" he crowed.

The guerrilla line started down the hill at a walk. Near the hollow, Anderson yelled, "Charge!" and the bushwhackers thundered up the opposite slope, screaming wildly and lying low in their saddles. They were still about 150 yards away when the anxious Federals opened fire. Shooting downhill may have thrown off the soldiers' aim, because nearly all the bullets whizzed harmlessly above the heads of the surging guerrillas. Only three bushwhackers were killed outright, and another later died of wounds received in the volley. Several others received minor wounds either in the initial barrage or in the close-quarters fighting that followed.

Anderson struck the Federal line with pistols blazing, and Todd and Thrailkill rushed out of the bottoms on either side of the field to join the charge. A screaming stampede was upon the Federals before they could reload their muskets. "The revolvers cracked rapidly," according to the *History of Boone County*, "so rapidly that the reports sounded at a distance like a heavy hail storm beating on glass roofs."

Many of the Federals fought valiantly, thrusting with their bayonets or wielding their muskets as clubs. Others, bowing to the guerrillas' demands to surrender, dropped to the ground and begged for mercy, but all met the same grim fate, a bullet through the head. Jesse James, according to his brother Frank, killed Major Johnston.

Anderson swept through the Federal line as planned and kept on toward the "fourth men." The horse holders offered little resistance. Some sat stunned and motionless in their saddles with their muskets across their laps until a guerrilla slug dropped them to the ground. A few dismounted and fired a single round before being overwhelmed. Most panicked and ran at the first charge. Releasing the mounts with which they had been entrusted, they turned and rode across the open prairie for Centralia, where they hoped to find safety.

For most, it was a futile race. As the *History of Boone County* notes, "the old sickle-hammed brood-mares and plow-horses, and the sore backed mules, were no matches in speed for the fine horses, the best in Missouri, ridden by the guerrillas." Out on the open prairie, the bushwhackers rode down the defenseless Federals one by one and dropped them to the grass with bullets through the brain. Fifteen fleeing soldiers were overtaken and killed between the battlefield and Centralia.

One officer, better mounted than most of his men, managed to reach Centralia and warn the soldiers who had been left in town under Captain Theis and Lieutenant Stafford. "Get out of here!" he shouted. "Every one of you will be killed if you don't."

Stafford and three of his men immediately started for Paris and managed to escape. Theis gathered the remainder of the company and headed for Sturgeon. As the formation marched out of town, four soldiers were shot from the ranks by a couple of bushwhackers lurking at the side of the road.

During Theis' hasty departure, some of the bluecoats were left behind. Dave Pool galloped into town at full speed and gunned down two stragglers near Sneed's Hotel. Other soldiers were found cowering in hiding places. The bushwhackers trailed one to the home of a sick lady and shot him dead as he cringed beside the woman's bed. They found two more perched in the outdoor toilet of the Eldorado House and killed them as they hunkered in the privy. They called another man out of the hotel with a promise of protection and shot him as he emerged.

The bloodthirsty guerrillas then set out on Theis' trail, chasing his company all the way to Sturgeon. One unfortunate soul died at the hand of Arch Clement just half a mile before his Union comrades finally found refuge in a Federal blockhouse.

Back at the battlefield, the victory celebration erupted into a circus of gore. The prisoner, Goodman, witnessed the gruesome scene and three years later still cringed at

> the bloody, dastardly, wanton acts committed upon the living and dead persons of those brave Union boys. Men's heads were severed from their lifeless bodies, exchanged as to bodies, labeled with rough and obscene epitaphs and inscriptions, stuck upon their carbine points, tied to their saddle bows, or sat grinning at each other from the tops of fence stakes and stumps.[4]

Official Union reports following the massacre mentioned still other indignities such as "noses cut off."[5] An officer at Macon, in a communication to General Fisk on September 29, two days after the atrocity, reported that "Ears were cut off and all commissioned officers were scalped" and "the privates cut from one wounded soldier while living and thrust in his mouth."[6]

In the brutal blood sport into which the guerrilla war in Missouri had degenerated by the fall of 1864, it was no longer enough merely to kill the enemy. Anderson and many of his men harbored such hatred for the Union that only the complete annihilation of the foe could satisfy their wild lust for vengeance. The mutilation of corpses was the grisly token of their craving to destroy the very identity and manhood of the Federals. The case of the castrated soldier whose genitals were crammed in his mouth was a literal manifestation of the guerrillas' aim of total emasculation of the enemy.

After the bushwhackers completed their butchery on the battlefield, they poured into Centralia on the heels of their comrades who had led the chase after the fleeing Federals. They discovered another stash of whiskey, and many celebrated their horrible victory by getting outrageously drunk for the second time that day. Anderson summoned Dr. Sneed to treat his wounded and ordered a local carpenter to make coffins for the three dead guerrillas, who were buried in a nearby cemetery.

After dark, the coarse mob paraded drunkenly back to camp at the Singleton farm. For the guerrillas the day had been an "extra occasion," as Goodman later overheard them call it.[7] Not only had they marched twenty-two Yankees off a train and shot them, they had completely demolished the Union force that had come out to redress the executions. Of Major Johnston's command of over 150 men, only about 25 managed to escape. True to his word, Anderson had shown that he could "kill men with as much rapidity and skill as anybody." Only Lawrence and Baxter Springs, among past guerrilla exploits, rivaled the atrocity, but Centralia topped them both in the number of Federal soldiers killed and in sheer brutality. It was Bill Anderson's greatest day!

CHAPTER THIRTEEN

I Could Not Throw My Life Away

Anderson and Todd allowed the guerrillas a brief rest at the Singleton farm before starting south late on the night of September 27. The procession included a wagon loaded with five or six wounded men and another piled high with weapons confiscated from the battlefield. After traveling about two miles, the guerrillas halted around midnight at a corn field surrounded by woods, where they fed their horses.[1]

At dawn on the 28th, the guerrillas marched another five miles and stopped again. From this camp, foraging parties went out in all directions, but before many provisions were brought in, a large Federal force under General Douglass came out from Columbia to spoil the scavenger hunt. The guerrillas fled precipitately as General Douglass pressed their retreat. The Federal advance and the guerrilla rear guard exchanged several shots, but the bushwhackers had no inclination to stop and make a stand against a well-armed force.

The Federals got close enough to fire a salvo from a six-pound artillery piece at the fleeing partisans, but the shells merely ripped through the leaves and branches of trees overhead, frightening the guerrillas momentarily but doing no real

Bill Anderson photographed approximately 1864.
—Used by permission, State Historical Society of Missouri, Columbia

damage. Striking a southwesterly course and traveling the woods rather than roads, the raiders broke into squads and pushed for their old haunts in Howard County.

Sergeant Goodman, provided with "an apology for shirt and breeches," was herded along with Anderson's squad.[2] In fear for his life at every turn, he was cursed, ill-treated, and made to go without food. At one point he was compelled to groom Anderson's horse, and after the job was finished, the chieftain spoke a few mild words to the captive. Anderson's passing notice leavened the hostility of the other guerrillas toward the prisoner, and his guards grew familiar. They shielded him from the torment of other bushwhackers and relaxed their scrutiny of his every movement.

Goodman acknowledged that the guerrilla command had more order and military deportment than he had expected, and he was impressed with Anderson's ability to control the behavior of "such a collection of wild, turbulent spirits" without mistreating them, all the while remaining on friendly terms with them.[3]

On the evening of the 28th, near Columbia, the guerrillas converged at a predesignated spot, an old hideout at a white church where they had a stockpile of food and whiskey stashed. One by one the various squads rode in, several of them fresh from skirmishes with the pursuing Union troops. The gathering erupted into a revel that appalled Goodman:

> By night nearly the whole command, Anderson and Todd included, were drunk even to madness. God help me, I never witnessed so much profanity in the same space of time before, or since. . . . They whooped, ran, jumped and yelled like so many savages. Once, Anderson, leaping on a horse, rode wildly through the crowd; firing his revolvers indiscriminately, and yelling like one possessed.[4]

The next morning Anderson appeared wearing a Federal officer's uniform, which had no doubt been taken from one of the dead bodies at Centralia, and he gave Goodman his old coat.

The guerrillas sobered up over a "council of war," during which they decided to split up and reassemble a few days later near Rocheport to cross the Missouri River. The countryside was swarming with Federals after the slaughter at Centralia. For the guerrillas to stay together in such a large body would be courting disaster, and operations north of the river would be difficult anyway. Anderson and Todd lingered briefly at the church with the twenty-man squad who had Goodman under guard before taking their leave.

Loyalist citizens and military authorities were outraged over Centralia, and during the next month many Southern sympathizers paid the consequences. On October 15, for example, Union soldiers killed fifteen "disloyal" citizens in eastern Randolph County and virtually destroyed the small village of Milton in retaliation for Anderson's deeds.

Indignation over Centralia was directed not just at Southern sympathizers and the bushwhackers themselves but also at the seeming inability of the Federal army to prevent such atrocities. General Fisk, in a communication to General Rosecrans, tried to answer such criticism:

> I am aware that it may seem to yourself and the impatient public remote from this section that we ought to accomplish more than we do; that the guerrillas ought to be exterminated from the country, and such disasters as those at Centralia prevented, but could you see this section of the State and study not only the topography of the country but the hearts and consciences of the people you would readily discover the great difficulties in the way of finding and exterminating bushwhackers.... Our movements, though made as secretly as possible, are discovered by the bushwhackers' friends and revealed from one to another. The citizens at home are our secret and most dangerous foes, and in no spot of all our disturbed territory has the rebellion more earnest friends than in the Missouri River counties of this district.[5]

As it had throughout the war, the network of civilian support decried by General Fisk aided the guerrillas during their flight from Centralia. From Glasgow on September 28, Fisk complained to his headquarters at St. Joseph, "Nearly every family in this infernal region has a representative either with Price's invading column or with Anderson in the brush."[6]

Anderson further frustrated the Union pursuit when he intercepted two dispatches sent to Fisk by officers involved in the chase and "read and returned them to the writers with his compliments."[7]

On the night of October 2, the squad guarding Goodman camped near Rocheport, close enough to watch flames dance in the sky above the town as the business district burned. Because of the town's Rebel sympathies and because the guerrillas were known to be in the surrounding area, Rocheport was under special Federal vigilance, but Fisk reported the blaze as "an accidental fire."[8]

Goodman's captors roamed in the area of the Boone-Howard county line for the next day or two. Then on October 4, the entire guerrilla command came together at its preappointed rendezvous, Harker's farm, located about four miles northeast of Rocheport. Here Anderson appeared and spoke briefly with his men, reassuring them that he would get them out of the area. After disbanding again, the guerrillas re-formed at the same place around noon on October 6 and started for the Missouri River.

The bushwhackers struck the river between Rocheport and Boonville and crossed to the south side by swimming their horses behind skiffs, which had been concealed in the nearby woods. Less than half the bushwhackers had crossed the river when some of the horses grew skittish about entering the water and neighed and reared in protest. The prisoner's guards, who had become increasingly lax in their watch, were momentarily distracted by the confusion, and Goodman simply walked past a group of unsuspecting guerrillas into some brush along the riverbank and made his escape.

After crossing the river, Anderson marched to Boonville to meet Price's army, while Todd ranged farther west into Johnson and Lafayette counties. General Price had failed in his aim to take the state capitol at Jefferson City and was retreating westward along the river. Despite the deterioration of his own troops' behavior during his march across Missouri, Old Pap was disgusted upon seeing the scalps dangling from the bridles of the guerrilla gang when he and Anderson met on October 11. Only after Anderson complied with an order to throw the hideous trophies away did the general warm to the partisan leader. He then accepted a pair of silver-mounted revolvers as a gift from the guerrilla chief and proclaimed that if he had fifty thousand men such as Anderson's crew he could hold Missouri permanently.

He decided, however, that the most practical service Anderson could render was the disruption of the movement of enemy troops and supplies by rail, and he thus issued the following "special order":

> Headquarters Army of Missouri
> Boonville, October 11, 1864
>
> Captain Anderson, with his command, will at once proceed to the north side of the Missouri River and permanently destroy the North Missouri Railroad, going as far east as practicable. He will report his operations at least every two days.
>
> By order of Major-General Price:
>
> McClean
> Lieutenant-Colonel and
> Assistant Adjutant-General[9]

Provided by Price with passage on a ferry boat, Anderson promptly recrossed the river to the north side. Once there, though, he made but a halfhearted effort to execute the general's order.

Riding seventy miles east with a band of about eighty men,

Anderson approached the town of Danville in Montgomery County at about nine o'clock on the evening of October 14.[10] There were no troops in the town, but the citizens were mainly Unionist, several of them having previously served in the army. With an assortment of shotguns, rifles, and other private arms, they had formed a sort of home guard, and they used a blockhouse near the square for the protection of the town. Some of these men were out on the street, discussing whether they needed to put out pickets for the night and place guards in the blockhouse, when Anderson's crew came galloping into town.[11]

Spotting the group, Anderson wheeled in the saddle and shouted to his men, "Fire on them!" The bushwhackers screamed and opened fire as they charged the citizens, killing two and scattering the rest. The guerrillas then proceeded to sack the town. They robbed private citizens, broke open stores and took whatever loot they wanted, and then sent nearly all the businesses and many houses up in flames. In the words of the anonymous author of *The History of St. Charles, Montgomery and Warren Counties*,

> Soon the whole town was one lurid glare of burning light. Vast clouds of black smoke rose in such density as to obscure the moon. Gusts and columns and jets of flame shot athwart the sky, and great showers of sparks and bits of burning wood were carried off and up into the canopy. All over town it was so light that one could see to pick up a pin.

When the alarm was first sounded, a doctor named Moore, who lived a few blocks away, started for the scene with his shotgun and a revolver, despite the pleas of his wife not to expose himself to danger. He dashed toward the first group of guerrillas he saw and opened fire, dropping one from the saddle with a serious wound. The rest of the gang turned on the man and filled him with lead, then battered his head with the butts of their guns to make sure he was dead.

A boy of ten or twelve years old sat in the doorway of his mother's house, watching the hellish scene in the streets of

Danville with youthful wonder, when a party of guerrillas rode by and spotted him. One member of the gang, apparently resentful of the boy's curiosity, took aim and shot him.

A group of the raiders visited the female academy that had recently been opened in Danville, but neither property nor person was hurt at the school. Some of the young women openly welcomed the guerrillas, claiming to be Rebels themselves, and by their actions probably prevented any damage that might otherwise have been done.

After a two-hour stay, the bushwhackers got ready to leave about eleven o'clock. Most of the prisoners they had gathered were released with a warning that they would be shot if they tried to leave town before sunup. Two other men were mounted double on a horse and forced to ride to the western edge of town, where one of them, named Simons, was dismounted. Arch Clement asked him whether he had ever been in the Union army, and he replied that he had, giving the name of his unit. Little Archie promptly raised up in the saddle and shot Simons to death.

From Danville, the bushwhackers rode on to New Florence, where they robbed the post office, stole some Federal uniforms from the train station, and then set the depot and two cars on fire. The county history suggests that no one died at New Florence, only because the place was such a small village and "no one could be found to kill."

From New Florence the guerrillas continued east to High Hill, arriving about sunrise on October 15. Again stores were broken into, citizens robbed, and the depot set ablaze. The gang found some whips in a saddle-and-harness shop and promptly tried them out on a few Union citizens.

The guerrillas rode out of High Hill and went into camp on a farm about three miles south of New Florence, where they took several passing farmers captive and forced them to supply the command with corn and other goods. Meanwhile, the Enrolled Missouri Militia at Wellsville had been informed of the sacking of Danville, and a detachment had set out in pursuit of the guerrillas. When the militiamen caught up to Anderson at his camp, their leader ordered a charge. The guerrillas retreated as soon as the firing began, but five of the captives, caught in the middle of the fray, were mistaken for Rebels and shot down by the zealous militia.

After being put to flight by the militia, Anderson and his band rode rapidly west without having accomplished the mission assigned by General Price. They had burned some depots but had failed to do any material harm to the railroad itself, as instructed by the general.

Price later complained that the guerrillas did do some damage but "totally failed in the main object proposed, which was to destroy the large railroad bridge that was in the end of St. Charles County."[12] Price neglected to mention, though, that Anderson had already brought normal traffic on the North Missouri Railroad to a halt with his raid at Centralia.

On October 15 the Federal garrison at Glasgow surrendered to General Shelby of Price's command. After the prisoners had been marched off to Boonville and Shelby had retired from the town, Anderson and his men, returning from Montgomery County, moved in to plunder. About ten o'clock on the night of October 21, Anderson and a companion named Berry visited the home of Benjamin W. Lewis, a wealthy citizen whose strong Unionist views made him a special target of the bushwhackers.

Lewis had even suggested to Federal officials that disloyal citizens in the area should be assessed a $5,000 fine. Apparently Bill Anderson had gotten wind of the statement and decided to turn the tables on Lewis by calling at the Unionist's home to assess a fine of sorts of his own.

Hammering at the door until it was finally opened, the two guerrillas barged in on Mrs. Lewis and two guests. Anderson and his sidekick demanded to see Mr. Lewis. At first Mrs. Lewis said her husband was not home, but the skeptical Anderson threatened to burn the house down if Lewis did not appear. Upon an assurance that her husband's life would be spared, Mrs. Lewis finally relented and summoned her husband from an upstairs room. While the bushwhackers waited for Lewis to appear, they helped themselves to dinner leftovers and washed them down with whiskey-laced wine. Anderson swigged the stuff so fast he began to hiccup.

When Lewis came downstairs, Anderson and Berry prodded him outdoors at gunpoint, cursing and shoving him along the way. Outside the house they knocked the fifty-year-old man to the ground with their pistols and threatened to kill him if he didn't hand over all the money he had.

They then herded Mr. Lewis back inside, where his wife produced about a thousand dollars in silver and paper, which was all the money in the house. Anderson ranted that there had to be more than that and resumed his torment of Lewis. He entertained himself by standing his victim against the wall and taking pot shots from across the room at Lewis' legs, miraculously hitting only the man's pants. Then he held his pistol near Lewis' knees and fired toward the man's bare feet. Anderson and Berry punched their victim in the ribs with their revolvers, and at one point both thrust the barrels of their pistols into Lewis' mouth at the same time. They laid him on his back and jumped on him, then lifted him up by his feet and dropped him on his head several times. Anderson punctuated the man's ordeal with an assortment of Indian yells that he identified by tribe.

Anderson, who knew Lewis had emancipated his slaves, turned to some of the man's servants. "You have been set free, have you?" he jibed.[13]

The blacks replied that they had.

Anderson spun back toward Lewis and struck him on the head with the muzzle of his revolver. "Yes, you damned old coon, you have set all your Negroes free."

At one point, according to a correspondent to the *St. Louis Daily Missouri Democrat,* Anderson and Berry violated a twelve- or thirteen-year-old black girl by turns. While the rape occurred, the one not immediately engaged in the licentious act kept up the torture of Lewis in a nearby room.

After several hours of torment, Lewis proposed to go to his neighbors and try to raise more money, and Anderson agreed. At about two in the morning, the three men set out toward town less than a mile away, and Lewis enlisted the help of two ladies in collecting more cash. Along the road to town, Anderson placed a bowie knife to his victim's throat and threatened to cut his jugular vein and also tried to trample Lewis beneath his horse, which he called "Sterling" in honor of General Price.

In town Anderson broke into a store, laid Lewis across a counter, and pulled out the bowie knife again. He slit open the terrified man's shirt and vest and was amusing himself by slicing his pants to pieces when one of the ladies showed up with $5,000, all the money she could find in town. Berry struck a bargain with her to release Lewis in exchange for the cash, and Anderson reluctantly accepted the deal. The woman whisked Lewis away before the two desperadoes could change their minds.[14]

The massacre at Centralia and the debauchery at Glasgow, particularly the rape of the black girl, were the crowning badge of Anderson's descent into savagery. Deeds he might have shunned just a few short years earlier were now accepted as a matter of course.

When Anderson left Glasgow about October 23, he had a force of 150 men. He marched north into Chariton, then swung west. He passed through Carroll County on the evening of the 24th and killed at least five Union men along the way. After killing a man named Etter, he took an old man named Eisenhour as a guide. Anderson told Eisenhour that the guerrillas were members of Jim Lane's Kansas jayhawkers, and the old man fell for the trick, admitting that he, too, was a strong Federal sympathizer.

According to the *History of Carroll County*, Anderson detailed three bushwhackers, Arch Clement included, "to take the guide to the rear and parole him."[15] The small squad took Eisenhour into some brush beside the road, threw him on the ground, and decapitated him. They searched the dead man's pockets, then set the bleeding head on the chest of the corpse and folded the arms across the body in such a manner that the headless man appeared to cradle his own head. The grim threesome then mounted up and rode away to join their fellow bushwhackers, who continued west into Ray County.

In their ambition to exterminate Bill Anderson, Union officials employed all available resources. Samuel P. "Cob" Cox, a veteran of the Mexican War and a major during the early stages of the Civil War before being sidelined by typhoid fever, had been called back into service without commission because, as Brig. Gen. James Craig later stated, "I believed he would find and whip Anderson."[16] On the morning of October 27, Major Cox, who was stationed at Richmond in central Ray County, got word from a local woman that Anderson was camped near the small village of Albany in the southwestern part of the county.[17]

Cox mounted 150 men of the Thirty-third and Fifty-first Enrolled Missouri Militia and set out on a hard march. About a mile east of Albany, Cox encountered the guerrilla pickets and drove them through the town and into the woods beyond.

Cox dismounted his men, formed them at the edge of the woods, and sent a cavalry advance ahead. The scouting party briefly engaged the bushwhackers, then fell back in much the same way Dave Pool had lured the Yankees into the clutches of the guerrillas at Singleton's farm.

Now the tables were turned, but Anderson was undaunted when he saw the Federal line. Perhaps the dismounted infantry with their Enfield rifles reminded him of Centralia. It was to be another slaughter! He shouted, "Charge!" and the guerrillas raised a wild chorus of Indian yells and fired their revolvers as their horses pounded toward the line.

But these were not Major Johnston's raw volunteers, and the guerrillas were bunched on a narrow lane surrounded by heavy woods rather than in an open field. When several of the bushwhackers fell in the first volley and the Federal line held firm, most of the guerrillas quickly drew rein.

Only Anderson and one other man, supposed to be a son of Confederate general James S. Rains, kept on coming. Despite bullets whizzing around them, they galloped through the line unscathed and appeared to make it to safety. Fifty paces to the Federal rear, though, Anderson was shot and toppled from the saddle with two balls in the side of the head.

Rains, unhorsed, managed to scramble off into some brush but was found dead the next day. The rest of the guerrillas were routed and chased down the road for nearly ten miles. Four of the gang besides Anderson had been killed outright, and the road taken by the guerrillas on their retreat was stained with the blood of numerous wounded. Militia losses were five or six wounded, one of whom died a couple of days later.

On the surface, the reckless act of abandon that brought Anderson's end was the headlong behavior of a maniac too sure of his own omnipotence, but the fragile shield of invincibility only disguised a deeper-seated death wish. According to Edwards, Anderson was known to have said on several occasions, "If I cared for my life I would have lost it long ago; wanting to lose it, I cannot throw it away."[18] He had finally tempted fate once too often.

CHAPTER FOURTEEN

One Devil Less in the World

The Federals searched Anderson's body and found six revolvers; about $600 in gold and treasury notes; orders from General Price; pictures of Anderson and his wife; a letter from his wife in Texas dated April 20, 1864, and signed "your ever loving and obedient wife until death"; a lock of her hair; a gold watch; a silver watch; and a small Confederate flag on which were inscribed the following words: "Presented to W. L. Anderson by his friend, F. M. R. Let it not be contaminated by Fed. hands."[1] According to legend, also found on the body was a silver cord with fifty-three knots, one for every Union man Anderson had killed in revenge for his sister's death. Found on Anderson's iron gray mare was a human scalp dangling from the bridle.

The corpse was loaded into a wagon and hauled to Richmond. After the body was rolled from the wagon, soldiers tied ropes around it and dragged it through the square behind their horses.[2] Some of the citizens were alarmed by such a scene and persuaded the Yankees to halt the exhibition.

The body was then placed on display at the courthouse. People reportedly came from miles around to view it, and some cut souvenir strands of hair from Anderson's flowing locks. The

One Devil Less in the World   137

Bill Anderson's body was displayed and photographs taken after his death.
—Used by permission, State Historical Society of Missouri, Columbia

body was recognized by several people who had known the guerrilla leader. With a revolver placed in its right hand, the corpse was propped up and tied to a chair so that the local photographer could take pictures of it, and for several days afterward, "likenesses" of the "notorious bushwhacker Bill Anderson" were offered to the public.[3]

The next day the body was buried in "a decent coffin" in the city cemetery at the northern edge of Richmond. One of Cox's men pointed out that the casket was "a respect due not to him, but to ourselves and to humanity."[4] The militiamen's spitting and urinating on the grave later that evening were a better indication of the soldiers' true feelings.

Cox was accorded hero's status for doing what no other Union officer in northern Missouri had been able to do. As a reward "for the distinguished service" he had "lately rendered his country," he was presented by Brig. Gen. James Craig with Anderson's horse and saddle, the small Confederate flag found on the body, and two of the six revolvers.[5] The other four pistols and the two watches were distributed among the other officers and men, and the money was given to those soldiers who were wounded in the fight and to the families of those killed.

In addition, General Craig, commander of the Seventh Military District of Missouri, issued an order of commendation through his adjutant general:

> The General tenders to Colonel Cox, and to the officers and men of his command engaged in this praiseworthy act, his heartfelt thanks and congratulations in ridding the country of such a blood-thirsty villain as Anderson, who has been for months past a terror to the loyal people of Missouri; and he feels satisfied that every well-wisher of his country will join in this congratulation, and that the blessings and prayers of many a disconsolate widow and orphan will ascend to Heaven for the future welfare of Colonel Cox and his brave band.
>
> This order will be read at the head of every command within the limits of this district, immediately after the receipt of this order.[6]

Cox also received, on November 30, 1864, his belated commission as a lieutenant colonel.

For forty-four years Anderson's body lay in the potter's field with very little public notice. Then on June 8, 1908, Cole Younger went to Richmond as part of a traveling carnival and learned that his old comrade was interred there. He was disturbed that Anderson had been buried without "proper respect," and he made arrangements for a funeral, which was held the next day.

The body of the guerrilla leader then lay without recognition for another six decades, and over the years, all signs of the burial place vanished. There were still those who remembered where it had been, however, and pictures taken about 1900 showed its location in reference to other landmarks. Kansas City area historian Donald R. Hale petitioned the government for a tombstone to mark Anderson's grave, a respect that by law is accorded to any veteran of any U.S. war. One April afternoon in 1967, Hale and his father unceremoniously placed a small granite stone to designate Bill Anderson's final resting place.

After Anderson's death, Arch Clement took command of the guerrilla band, but Little Archie's pure viciousness was no substitute for Anderson's impassioned hatred of the enemy. Without the reckless spirit of Anderson to drive them, the gang soon fragmented. The guerrillas split into small groups, joined other leaders, or slipped down into Texas to pass the winter.

Anderson's death (coming six days after Todd had been killed near Kansas City) revived the ambitions of Quantrill, and in the winter of 1864–65 he led about forty guerrillas on an ill-fated journey to Kentucky, where he was mortally wounded on May 10, 1865, a month after Lee's surrender at Appomattox. On May 21 Dave Pool, in command of forty men, consisting of parts of Anderson's and Todd's bands, surrendered at Lexington, Missouri. Others, like Jim Anderson and Clement, who still commanded a remnant of Bill Anderson's band, held out to the bitter end. Both died violently after the close of the war. Clement was riddled with bullets by militiamen at Lexington after he shot up a saloon there in December of 1866,

Bill Anderson's gravesite in the Richmond, Missouri, Pioneer Cemetery, five blocks north of the town square.

and the following spring Jim Anderson had his throat cut on the lawn of the courthouse at Sherman, Texas, by a former guerrilla.

During Bill Anderson's own time, Unionists called him a devil, an "incarnate fiend," and other demonizing terms.[7] The *Columbia Missouri Statesman* avowed that he and his followers were "inhuman butchers, in whose hearts does not exist the faintest spark of moral feeling or of mercy."[8] The *St. Louis Daily Missouri Democrat,* in describing Centralia, said, "In brutality and fiendishness these horrible deeds were never surpassed."[9] A correspondent for the same paper, in describing the torture of Benjamin Lewis at Glasgow, attributed the deed to "the monster Bill Anderson, . . . whom I solemnly believe to be without parallel in the history of crime."[10] General Fisk, in reference to the various guerrilla leaders, said simply that Anderson was "the worst of all."[11]

Observers were no less restrained during the first half-century after Anderson's death. To Edwards, who had served during the war as General Shelby's adjutant, Anderson was an avenging "giant" who fought and died heroically. Connelley, on the other hand, portrayed Anderson as a hardened criminal of base character long before the Civil War began.

Recent writers have tended to avoid emotional language in favor of more objective assessment. One historian, for example, says simply of Anderson, "Between July and October [1864] he made more raids, rode more miles, and killed more men than any other guerrilla chieftain, including Quantrill, ever did."[12]

Anderson probably would have led a life of horse thievery and petty crime in any case, but it is safe to say that fate and circumstance drastically changed the course of his life. A war that at first he was not eager to fight turned him at last into a monster. Frightened Union citizens in the border state of Missouri and dignitaries on both sides responsible for governing the conflict were horrified that there were those like William T. Anderson who would not fight it by "civilized" rules. Before it was over, Anderson had become the bloodiest man in America's deadliest war.

Notes

In citing works in the notes, I have generally used short titles. Sources frequently cited are identified by the following abbreviations:

Border Wars	William E. Connelley. *Quantrill and the Border Wars*. Cedar Rapids (IA): The Torch Press, 1910.
CMS	*Columbia Missouri Statesman*.
HBC	*History of Boone County*. St. Louis: Western Historical Company, 1882.
HCC	*History of Carroll County*. St. Louis: Missouri Historical Company, 1881.
KCDJC	*Kansas City Daily Journal of Commerce*.
KSHS	Kansas State Historical Society, Topeka.
MHR	*Missouri Historical Review*.
OR	*War of the Rebellion: A Compilation of Official Records of the Union and Confederate Armies*. Washington, D. C.: Government Printing Office, 1880-1902. (All references are to Series 1 unless otherwise stated.)

CHAPTER ONE—**My Native State of Missouri**

The first part of the book title is taken from Anderson's manifesto delivered to Lexington, Missouri, newspapers during the summer of 1864. Unless otherwise stated, all chapter titles are taken from the same source.

1. Bill Anderson's exact date of birth is unknown, and conflicting evidence also exists as to his place of birth. The 1850 census of Randolph

County, Missouri, lists the birthplace of all the Anderson children as Missouri, and in his manifesto written in the summer of 1864, Anderson calls Missouri his native state. Also, it is known that the family lived at Palmyra, Missouri, when Bill was an infant (see 1840 Marion County census).

However, the 1860 census of Breckinridge County, Kansas, lists Kentucky as the birthplace of Bill Anderson, Iowa as the birthplace of his brother Jim, and Missouri as the birthplace of their sisters. (Ellis Anderson, the second-born child, is missing from the 1860 census, as he had already died or left home. A fourth brother, Charles, was born after the family moved to Kansas and is listed on the census as one year old.)

The Iowa connection is supported by the recollection of an Anderson neighbor in Kansas that the family had lived in Iowa Territory before moving to Missouri and then on to Kansas. Also, a series of ads soliciting animal pelts, placed by Thomasson in the *Palmyra Missouri Whig and General Advertiser*, ran from the fall of 1840 until the spring of 1841 and were then discontinued, indicating that he and the Andersons may have moved shortly thereafter. So, the most likely scenario seems to be that the family moved from Kentucky to Missouri shortly after Bill's birth, to Iowa after the spring of 1841, and back to Missouri prior to Mary Anderson's birth.

Both the 1850 census and the 1860 census assign Kentucky as the native state of William C. Anderson and his wife, Martha. (Martha's parents, William Thomasson and Mahala Baker, were married in Hopkins County in 1818.)

2. Sources vary concerning the names of the Anderson sisters. In determining their names I've supplemented a study of census records with information gained from other sources. Mary, whose middle name was Ellen, was often called by the nickname Molly. Josephine was sometimes called Josie. Martha was occasionally called by the nickname Mattie. Sources also refer to her variously as Janie or Jennie. Since her middle initial is known to have been "J," I've ascribed to her the full name Martha Jane as more likely than Martha Jennie.

3. The Tad Austin quote concerning Bill Anderson's quiet manner as a child is taken from a 1 October 1899 *St. Louis Republic* newspaper article entitled "When Bill Anderson the Guerrilla Was at Huntsville." This article also provides some of the other background on Anderson's early life in Missouri.

4. The 1859 Kansas Territorial Census gives the year of William C. Anderson's settlement in the territory as 1857, and information from other sources seems to confirm this date.

5. The 1840 census shows that the Andersons had one black female under the age of ten living in their household, but ten years later the family owned no slaves. William C. Anderson's name does not appear on the 1850 Slave Schedule for Randolph County, Missouri.

6. The L. D. Bailey quote classifying the Andersons as "a rough type" is from Charles Green's *Early Days in Kansas*, 1:45. See Fellman's *Inside War* for a thoughtful analysis of the stereotypes that Northerners and Missourians held of each other during the struggle for "Bleeding Kansas."

7. Cutler's *History of the State of Kansas*, 2:847.

8. Eli Sewell's statement that Bill Anderson was a "steady boy" is found in the William Connelley papers, Box 13, at the KSHS. These papers, Green's *Early Days,* and contemporaneous accounts from Kansas newspapers are the primary sources for information concerning Anderson's life in Kansas.

CHAPTER TWO—They Murdered My Father

1. The quote about jayhawkers overrunning western Missouri is from Mrs. Upton Hays in Albert Doerschuk's "Extracts of War Time-Time Letters, 1861-1864," MHR 23 (October 1928): 100. Goodrich's *Black Flag* provides some of the background about general conditions along the border during the first year of the war. See also Castel's "Kansas Jayhawking Raids into Western Missouri in 1861," MHR 54 (October 1959): 1-11.

2. Eli Sewell, whose ranch the Anderson brothers stayed on, is the source (in the Connelley papers) for both tales concerning the brothers' separate run-ins with Indians. He recalled the incidents as an old man many years later. However, he offers convincing specifics, and his accounts of other episodes seem credible.

His stories are confirmed by John Maloy's "History of Morris County" in the 7 May 1886 edition of the *Kansas Cosmos,* in which the author recalls that the Anderson brothers "wantonly murdered two or three Indians, and for some reason were not held to answer for their crimes before the law." C. H. Strieby (also in the Connelley papers) further confirms that Ellis Anderson had some sort of clash with Indians. He claims that Anderson himself was killed by Indians. A conflicting report (Castel and Goodrich, *Bloody Bill Anderson,* p. 146) suggests that Ellis Anderson lived to produce children through whom he has descendants today; however, there's no trace of Anderson anywhere in the United States in the 1860 or 1870 census.

So, the incidents involving the Anderson brothers' separate run-ins with Indians, while not widely reported, seem to have some basis in fact. Tension between white settlers and Kaw Indians, whose reservation encompassed the town of Council Grove, ran high in frontier Kansas. Clashes between the two sides were not uncommon. In such an atmosphere, the death of an Indian or two was not a cause for great alarm among settlers unless the Indians grew hostile in return.

3. Freighting along the Santa Fe Road boomed during the time the Andersons lived in Kansas. During one two-month period in the spring of 1860, 2,004 men, 1,400 wagons, 372 horses, 3,868 mules, 11,705 oxen, and 65 carriages passed Council Grove in trains to and from New Mexico, carrying 3,562 tons of freight. Charlie Parker, the man with whom the Andersons were associated, passed through in mid-March of 1860, headed for Kansas City with 20 wagons loaded with Mexican wool, 2 carriages, 1 buggy, 1 ambulance, 240 mules, 30 men, and 14 passengers.

4. As early as June of 1859, S. N. Wood, editor of the *Kansas Press* (later the *Council Grove Press*), complained of organized gangs of horse thieves "extending from Council Grove to the state of Missouri." There's no evidence, however,

that Bill Anderson was involved in the gangs at this date. The Anderson family appears to have still been in good standing with the community at least as late as December of 1859, when Bill's father was a charter member of the Morris County Frontier Rifle Guards, a military company organized in the Council Grove area for the protection of white settlers from Indians.

5. "Lee" Griffin and "Bert" Griffin are alternately mentioned in connection with Bill Anderson and A. I. Baker. A seventeen-year-old named Albert Griffin lived at Rock Creek with A. I. Baker at the time of the 1860 Breckinridge County census. Evidence suggests that Lee and Albert "Bert" Griffin were the same person and that his full name was Albert Leander Griffin or Albert Leonidas Griffin.

6. Strieby's recollection that Bill Anderson cared nothing for the South is in the Connelley papers.

7. During the late 1850s A. I. Baker was active in the founding of the Republican Party in Breckinridge County, but by late 1859 he was under attack from his own party for aligning himself with free-state Democrats (who opposed Negroes, free or slave, coming to Kansas). As late as the fall of 1861, Baker still avowed his support for the Union (see *Emporia News* of the period), but he also maintained an unflagging defense of slavery. His ill-fated attempt to join the Missouri State Guard forces indicates that the latter sentiment may have been a little stronger than the former.

Other authors have suggested that the trip to Missouri was just a jayhawking expedition rather than an effort to enlist in the army, but a preponderance of evidence supports the latter conclusion (e.g. 7 December 1861 *Emporia News*, 2 January 1862 *White Cloud Kansas Chief*, 7 May 1886 *Kansas Cosmos*, the Connelley papers, and General Price's call for recruits in OR, vol. 8, 693-697).

8. *Kansas Cosmos*, 7 May 1886 and 1860 Jasper County, Missouri, census.

9. Breckinridge County had originally been named for John C. Breckinridge, vice president under Lincoln's Democratic predecessor, James Buchanan. The name change to Lyon County was an obvious political statement. Just prior to the change, the editor of the *Emporia News* declared, "We don't want our county named after the traitor, Breckinridge."

10. The description of Molly Anderson as a "bitter rebel" is by Strieby in the Connelley papers.

11. Baker concluded his April 1862 letter to the *Emporia News*, in which he sought to regain favor with the people of the county, with the following lines borrowed from Lord Byron:

> Here's a sigh to those who love me,
> And a smile to those who hate;
> And, whatsoever sky's above me,
> Here's a heart for every fate.

In an ironic twist, Quantrill pilfered the same lines for a poem he penned and gave to a Kentucky girl in February of 1865. Like Baker, he was killed shortly after inscribing the fateful stanza.

12. O'Dell's description of Bill Anderson's horse as the "fastest in the Western states" is in Green's *Early Days*, 1:48.

13. *Emporia News*, 12 July 1862. The *Junction City Smoky Hill and Republican Union*, 29 May 1862, also makes clear that Anderson's motives for trying to kill Baker were more personal than political.

14. The *Smoky Hill and Republican Union*, 29 May 1862, reported that Anderson fired first but that the constable shoved aside the barrel of his gun, diverting it from its target.

15. A variation on the story of the killing of Bill Anderson's father says that the shooting occurred on the wedding day of A. I. Baker and Annis Segur. The source for this embellishment is the account in Green's *Early Days* of L. D. Bailey, an attorney who lived in Emporia about twenty miles away and who recalled the incident of the "bloody nuptials" almost fifty years later. Morris County, Kansas, marriage records, however, show the wedding occurred on May 14, two days after the death of William C. Anderson.

CHAPTER THREE—The Last Man You Ever Will See

The chapter title is part of what Anderson supposedly said to Judge Baker before killing him, as recounted by B. F. Munkers in the Connelley papers at the KSHS.

1. The Gregg quote about the first time he saw Anderson appears in the *Kansas City Journal*, 12 May 1888.

2. Reed, like Lee Griffin, was reportedly a cousin of the Andersons (Green's *Early Days*, 1:48-51). The home near the Missouri border where the Anderson girls stayed when they fled the Council Grove area may have been that of a man named Solomon Reed (see 1860 Wyandotte County, Kansas, census). Numerous claims of kinship with Bill Anderson surfaced after the war, however, and many of them were undoubtedly false. I've found no evidence that any Anderson family besides that of William C. Anderson or any Thomasson family besides that of William Thomasson came to Missouri from Hopkins County, Kentucky, with these two families. I've also found no marriage record during the correct time frame involving the surname Anderson or the surname Thomasson linked with any of the surnames of the supposed "cousins" of Bill Anderson in the locations where the Anderson family was known to have lived.

3. Some reports claim that Quantrill himself was along on the raid in which A. I. Baker was killed. However, at the time, Quantrill was otherwise engaged. In late June, at the request of Missouri State Guard colonel Upton Hays, Quantrill led a large group of his men south from Jackson County into Henry County (Missouri), and during the return trip in early July, Quantrill fought with Federal troops near Pleasant Hill in Cass County. Also, no former Quantrill guerrilla nor serious Quantrill biographer makes the claim that Quantrill accompanied Anderson. It was made by a few Kansans who knew Anderson and

by one who claimed to have known Quantrill. Even some of the Kansans who knew Anderson, however, denied the story's validity. False Quantrill sightings were common by the summer of 1862, especially in Kansas.

4. The reported verbal exchange between Anderson and Baker just prior to Baker's death, as recounted by Munkers in the Connelley papers, has the tone of romantic legend. However, the conversation could have some basis in fact, since Baker's brother-in-law lived long enough to relate the circumstances of the assault.

CHAPTER FOUR—The Most Desperate of Desperate Men
  The title is taken from Cole Younger's book *Cole Younger by Himself.*
  1. *History of Lafayette County, Missouri*, 481.
  2. *Lexington (Missouri) Weekly Union*, 7 February 1863.
  3. The winter 1961 issue of *Frontier Times* recounts another fictitious tale that, like the story of Quantrill helping to murder Baker, places the date of Bill Anderson joining Quantrill earlier than the alliance actually occurred. When Union forces were detached to Aubrey, Kansas, to investigate after Quantrill's March 7, 1862, raid on the small village, the story claims, they were furnished with a list of Confederate sympathizers on which appeared the names of Bill Anderson's father and uncle. A squad of troops sent to the Anderson home three miles from Aubrey hanged the two men on March 11. Bill and his brother Jim were away from home but learned of the shocking news upon their return the following day. That night, Bill began his "campaign of murder" near Aubrey when he slipped up behind a Union picket and broke his neck. The next night, he killed two more soldiers, then fled to Missouri. John McCorkle found him sleeping in the barn of a Confederate sympathizer named George Reed, and, after a tense standoff between the two men, recruited Anderson to Quantrill's band.

  This yarn is obvious fantasy. Anderson's father was not hanged by Union troops, he didn't die in March of 1862, and he lived nowhere near Aubrey. Also, McCorkle himself did not join Quantrill until the summer of 1862. One thread of truth to the story may be Anderson's connection to George Reed, the Southern sympathizer, because it is known that a man named Reed took part in the killing of A. I. Baker.

  4. The physical description of Anderson, including the brief quotes, is drawn from Richard Cordley's *A History of Lawrence*, p. 199, and from the *St. Louis Democrat*, 11 November 1864. See also Edwards' *Noted Guerrillas*, 166, and Goodman's *Thrilling Record*, 29-30.
  5. *Cole Younger by Himself.*
  6. The account of the Yeager raid is taken largely from the *Emporia News*, 9 May 1863 and 16 May 1863. Griffin, as well as Anderson, was reportedly recognized by Kansans during this raid, but according to the *Lexington Weekly Union*, Griffin was already dead. It's possible, however, that the *Weekly Union* account was mistaken and that Reed, not Griffin, was the one who had been killed.
  7. *KCDJC*, 16 May 1863.

8. Authority for Anderson's rank as a lieutenant under Todd in the Quantrill command structure is Cole Younger's story in the *Kansas City Post*, 21 March 1915, and Edwards, *Noted Guerrillas*.

9. The *Lexington Union* story about Anderson and Pool's raid in Lafayette County is quoted in the *KCDJC*, 23 July 1863.

10. *OR*, vol. 22, pt. 2, 377-378.

11. The main source for Anderson's July 31, 1863, raid along the Shawnee Road is the *KCDJC*, 2 August and 7 August 1863. See also the 1 August 1863 *Wyandotte Commercial Gazette*, the 2 August and 4 August 1863 *Leavenworth Conservative*, and Connelley's *The Life of Preston B. Plumb*.

CHAPTER FIVE—They Murdered My Sister

1. Principal sources for the details surrounding the Union roundup of the Anderson girls are Connelley's *Border Wars* and the Connelley papers at the KSHS. See also an undated newspaper clipping entitled "Bill Anderson and Not Charlie Quantrell Was Driving Force Behind Lawrence Raid" in the Connelley collection at the Denver Public Library's Western History Department.

2. Previous authors have varied widely in assigning ages to Bill Anderson's sisters. I have derived their ages from the 1850 and 1860 census records. The two sources are in general agreement on the ages of Mary and Josephine. However, the 1860 census lists Martha's age as eight. This is an obvious error, since she was listed as five months old in 1850. She had to be at least ten in 1860 and, therefore, had to be at least thirteen in 1863 at the time of the prison collapse, not ten as many authors have said.

3. Some authors have said that Molly Anderson was seriously wounded in the collapse, too, but there seems to be little evidence to support this. McCorkle (*Three Years with Quantrill*, p. 122) says that Molly Anderson and Nannie Harris were carried to safety by a guard and clearly implies that they were not seriously injured. Also, the 15 August 1863 *KCDJC* names, in addition to the dead girls, only two additional victims: Mattie Anderson, badly wounded, and Mollie Grandstaff, slightly wounded.

4. Leslie, *The Devil Knows How to Ride*, 194-198.

5. See Harris', "Catalyst for Terror: The Collapse of the Women's Prison in Kansas City," for a thorough discussion of the collapse and its cause.

6. Barton, *Three Years with Quantrill*, 120.

7. In addition to the other four family members who died between 1859 and 1863, Bill's infant brother Charles may also have died during this period, since there seems to be no trace of him beyond the 1860 census.

8. Brownlee, *Gray Ghosts of the Confederacy*, 119-120.

9. Edwards, *Noted Guerrillas*, 189.

10. *OR*, vol. 22, pt. 2, 460-461.

CHAPTER SIX—I Have Glutted My Vengeance

1. Connelley, *Border Wars*, and Leslie, *The Devil Knows How to Ride*, provide

much of the general background concerning the ride to Lawrence and the sacking of the town, although I also consulted numerous other sources.

2. Gregg, "The Lawrence Raid," typescript manuscript in Civil War Narratives at the KSHS.

3. Anderson's chance meeting with Benjamin O'Dell: Green's *Early Days*, 1:51.

4. Gregg, *A Little Dab of History without Embelishment*, 59.

5. Anderson taking Captain Banks' uniform: 29 August 1863 *Emporia News* citing a *Leavenworth Daily Conservative* correspondent. An account in Shea's *Reminiscences*, however, has Todd wearing the uniform later in the morning.

6. The story involving Getta Dix, including the quotations, is from "Quantrill's Raid, an Eyewitness Account," *Westport Historical Quarterly*, May 1965. The events at Lawrence that I've chosen to depict are meant only to suggest the atmosphere of the carnage and not to imply Anderson's direct participation, unless specifically stated.

7. Anderson sparing the Grovenor home, including the quote: account of L. D. Bailey in Shea's *Reminiscences*, 45-46.

8. The incident at the Bullene residence, including Anderson's quotes: account of William L. Bullene in Shea's *Reminiscences*, 25-26. Although Anderson is never specifically identified by name, the statement made by the guerrilla suggests the speaker was probably Anderson.

9. Anderson's conversation with Mrs. Grovenor as the guerrillas were gathering to leave: *Border Wars*, 364.

10. Edwards, *Noted Guerillas*, 193.

11. *Border Wars*, 384.

CHAPTER SEVEN—Quantrill's Sand Is Gone

The title is one of several derogatory comments, as reported by Connelley, that Anderson and Todd made about Quantrill during the summer of 1864.

1. The quote about killing all the preachers is recounted in *Border Wars*, 383.

2. Captain Coleman's report, *OR*, vol. 22, pt. 1, 590.

3. The Bledsoe incident and his comment about not expecting mercy: *Border Wars*, 415-416.

4. Blunt's comment about the scalped guerrillas is quoted in Edwards, *Noted Guerillas*, 207, but the author says the remark was in reference to Ab Haller, not Bledsoe.

5. Lazear's letter to his wife: *MHR* 45 (July 1950): 391.

6. Quantrill getting drunk on Blunt's whiskey is recounted in Connelley's interview with Gregg in the Connelley papers at the KSHS.

7. Riley Crawford shooting the soldier who had been playing possum: *Border Wars*, 430.

8. Report of W. C. Quantrill, *OR*, vol. 22, pt. 1, 701.

9. Gregg, *A Little Dab*, 87.

10. Whether Anderson and Bush Smith were ever actually married was a question of debate for some time, but it is now an accepted fact. McCorkle (*Three Years with Quantrill*) said the wedding took place during Christmas week, but the marriage certificate, filed in Grayson County, Texas, shows the license was issued on 2 March 1864, and the ceremony performed on 3 March by M. J. Brackett, Minister of the Gospel.

11. Anderson's break with Quantrill: *Border Wars* and Castel, *William Clarke Quantrill*.

12. Quantrill's conversation with McCulloch and escape from Bonham: *Border Wars*, 443. See also David Paul Smith, "William Clarke Quantrill," *The Handbook of Texas Online*, www.tsha.utexas.edu/handbook/online/articles/print/QQ/fqu3.html.

13. Anderson's skirmish with Todd: *Border Wars*, 444.

14. Whether Anderson received a commission from Price after his split from Quantrill is not certain. Monaghan (*Civil War on the Western Border, 1854-1865*) says that he did, and Price referred to Anderson as "Captain" in written correspondence during the summer of 1864. During the same summer, Anderson likewise referred to himself as a captain, whereas at the time of his marriage, while he was still in Quantrill's command, he had called himself a lieutenant. However, in July of 1864 he also denied ever having belonged to the Confederate army. The issue of whether Anderson and other guerrilla leaders were acting with official Confederate sanction was a prominent question in the minds of Unionists even during the war.

CHAPTER EIGHT—I Had Them to Kill

1. *History of Greene County, Missouri*, 472-473. Although this 1883 report is unsubstantiated by available contemporaneous sources, the time frame and circumstances described in the account seem convincing.

2. The account of the Cooper County raid is drawn largely from the *Boonville Weekly Monitor*, 11 June 1864. See also Levens and Drake's 1876 *A History of Cooper County*; *OR*, vol. 34, pt. 4, 235 and 238; and the 1860 Cooper County census.

3. Higbee's name is spelled "Higby" in the newspaper account and the county history, but the only man with a similar name who is known to have ridden with Quantrill was Charles Higbee.

4. *OR*, vol. 34, pt. 3, 186.

5. *OR*, vol. 34, pt. 1, 1001-1002.

6. Edwards and former guerrillas (e.g. Younger) claimed, apparently with some validity, that the bushwhackers scalped by the Union during the retreat from Lawrence represented the first instances of scalping. Both sides used the practice with increasing regularity during the summer of 1864. However, scalping became the special mark of Anderson's gang because of the band's frequent use of the technique and its propensity for displaying the scalps.

7. The kidnapping of the postmaster at Wellington: *OR*, vol. 34, pt. 4, 564, and *St. Joseph Morning Herald*, 8 July 1864.

8. The attack on the Live Oak, including the brief quotes: *Carrolton Democrat*, 8 July 1864.

9. Anderson's letters: *OR*, vol. 41, pt. 2, 75-77.

10. The 22 July 1864 *CMS* reported that Anna Fickle was sentenced by a military commission to three years at the Alton military prison. The 2 September issue of the same paper said she was sentenced to ten years in the state prison at Jefferson City.

11. The *HCC* published in 1881 places the date of the river crossing as Tuesday, July 11, and most authors since have accepted the 11th as the correct date. However, the 11th fell on a Monday, not a Tuesday. Furthermore, the 22 July 1864 *CMS* reported the crossing as having occurred on the 12th. So Tuesday the 12th is probably the correct date.

12. The main source for the raid through Carroll County, including the reconstructed dialogue, is the *HCC*. See also the July 15, 1864, *Carrolton Democrat*.

13. *CMS*, 22 July 1864.

Chapter Nine—Things I Would Shrink from If Possible to Avoid

1. Most reports say Anderson had about thirty-five men with him at Huntsville, whereas he had only twenty-one during his raid through Carroll County just a few days earlier, and back in Lafayette County he had only twelve until he joined forces with Yeager. The number of bushwhackers in Anderson's band during the summer of 1864 varied from a mere handful to well over a hundred. The guerrillas came and went as they pleased except in the face of battle, and smaller bands often splintered off from the main group.

2. The conversation between Anderson and his old acquaintance Tad Austin: "When Bill Anderson the Guerrilla Was at Huntsville," in the 1 October 1899 *St. Louis Republic*.

3. Quotes concerning the Huntsville raid that do not involve Tad Austin are taken from the *Huntsville Citizen*'s account of events as reprinted in the *CMS*, 29 July 1864. This account also provides most of the general description of the raid.

4. Quoted in Goodrich's *Black Flag*, 137.

5. The 29 July 1864 *CMS* is the source not only for this quote but in large part for the general account of the fight at Allen. The 5 August 1864 issue of the same paper is the main source for the fight after Anderson was driven out of Allen.

6. *OR*, vol. 41, pt. 2, 411.

7. Ibid., 479.

8. Ibid., 410.

9. *History of Monroe and Shelby Counties*, 769.

10. Ibid., 770.

11. This and succeeding dialogue pertaining to Anderson's second raid through Carroll County is taken from the *HCC*, which is also the main source for the general account of events. See, too, the 12 August 1864 *Carrollton Democrat*, the 19 August 1864 *CMS*, and the 1860 Carroll County census.

12. The 1881 *HCC* says the bushwhackers stopped at the Mitchell farm and demanded "dinner," a colloquialism denoting the noon meal. According to the same history, the Anderson gang crossed into Carroll County during the morning and arrived at the Mitchell farm after a hard ride. Since the farm was only a few miles from the county line, the guerrillas probably arrived around midday, not in the late afternoon or early evening as previous authors have implied.

13. Edwards says in *Noted Guerrillas* that Anderson shot Mrs. Mitchell accidentally.

CHAPTER TEN—I Will Hunt You Down Like Wolves

1. *HCC*, 350. The dialogue that follows this quote is taken from the same source.

2. *Liberty Tribune*, 12 August 1864.

3. *History of Clay and Platte Counties*, 253. See also *Caldwell County Banner of Liberty*, 19 August 1864.

4. *OR*, vol. 41, pt. 2, 690.

5. Ibid.

6. *HCC*, 352. The dialogue preceding the quote comes from the same source.

7. Ibid., 354.

8. *OR*, vol. 41, pt. 1, 252.

9. *OR*, vol. 41, pt. 3, 348.

10. Brownlee credits Anderson with the attack on the Omaha, but there seems to be no solid documentation of this.

11. *OR*, vol. 41, pt. 2, 858.

12. Ibid., 839.

13. Ibid.

14. *OR*, vol. 41, pt. 3, 396.

15. Brownlee, *Gray Ghosts of the Confederacy*, 211.

16. Ibid., 212.

17. *CMS*, September 9, 1864, and Barth papers, Western Historical Manuscript Collection, University of Missouri-Columbia, 7 September 1864 letter from John Hartman to Moses Barth.

18. *CMS*, 16 September 1864.

19. A Union communication of September 20 places a portion of Anderson's gang in St. Catharine, Linn County, on the 19th while Anderson and his men were actually operating in Howard County sixty miles away. If any Anderson men were at St. Catharine, they must have been a part of Jim Anderson's band and the source for the report simply failed to distinguish between the two brothers.

20. Watts, *Babe of the Company*, 10.

21. *Brunswick (Mo.) Brunswicker*, 30 September 1982.

22. Subsequent authors have generally perpetuated the original report that Anderson led the September 23 raid on the Federal wagon train north of

Rocheport. One notable exception is the author of the 1882 *HBC*, who states explicitly that Anderson was not there. Edwards credits Todd with the raid and clearly implies that Anderson was not there. Although generally unreliable, Edwards is correct in this case. Hamp Watts makes no mention of Anderson's company having participated in the raid and says that on the evening before the Fayette attack (when the wagon train raid occurred) Anderson was gathering his men in Howard County after they had been operating in small bands throughout most of the month. Also, Todd's men who later discussed or wrote about their experiences (e.g. McCorkle, Frank Smith) imply that Anderson was not at the raid on the wagon train.

Some authors have further suggested that the six members of Anderson's band who were scalped were killed during the Union pursuit after the raid on the wagon train. The scalping may have been an act of retaliation, but not for the wagon train raid. Even official Union records suggest that the killing of Anderson's men happened before the attack on the wagon train.

23. *OR*, vol. 41, pt. 1, 923.
24. Quoted in *Border Wars*, 453.
25. Watts, *Babe of the Company*, 13.
26. Ibid., 14.
27. *History of Howard and Chariton Counties*, 284.
28. Watts, *Babe of the Company*, 14.
29. *Columbia Missouri Herald*, 24 September 1897.
30. *OR*, vol. 41, pt. 1, 416.
31. At least one report suggests that Anderson and Todd split after the Fayette fiasco and reunited a few days later near Centralia. The preponderance of evidence, however, suggests that they stayed together throughout those few days.
32. *OR*, vol. 41, pt. 3, 394.
33. *OR*, vol. 41, pt. 1, 416.
34. *HBC*, 440.

CHAPTER ELEVEN—Every Federal Soldier Shall Die Like a Dog

The title is borrowed from an eyewitness account (in the *St. Joseph Morning Herald*) of the speech Anderson made to the soldiers before they were executed.

1. *HBC*, 443. The county history contains perhaps the most thorough original account of the Centralia massacre. All succeeding quotes in this chapter, including dialogue, are taken from the county history, except where otherwise noted.
2. *Kansas City Post*, 14 September 1907.
3. Ibid.
4. Reports differ as to whether any civilian passengers were killed during the initial barrage fired at the train as it stopped at the Centralia depot. The 30 September 1864 *CMS*, for instance, reported that two men were killed by stray bullets, but the *St. Louis Republican* of the same date said the salvo was aimed exclusively at the cab and that no passengers were killed.

5. *Kansas City Post*, 14 September 1907.
6. Ibid.
7. Reports also differ on how many people were shot deliberately prior to the execution of the soldiers. Various sources agree concerning the young man who was killed when he admitted concealing money in his boot. Another report says that Anderson shot a civilian down for resisting orders to disembark while the man was still on the train. A variation says that two soldiers were gunned down for similar reason.

While the various reports of individuals being killed prior to the execution of the soldiers differ in details, the prevalence of such reports suggests that probably one or more individuals besides the young man who hid his money were killed on the train, either intentionally or by stray bullets.

8. The *HBC* says that Frank James participated in the Centralia raid, a charge that James denied in an 1897 newspaper article. He said he was with Todd during the battle with Johnston's troops but was not at Centralia that morning. Although James rode east from Clay County with Anderson in August and participated in the fight in which his brother Jesse was seriously wounded, he was associated with Todd at least as closely as with Anderson. According to Edwards, the James brothers had gone back to the western part of the state and rendezvoused with Todd after Jesse's convalescence. So, Frank's denial that he was with Anderson in Centralia may have some credence.

9. *St. Joseph Morning Herald*, 30 September 1864.
10. Ibid.
11. Sgt. Thomas Goodman, *A Thrilling Record*, 24.
12. Ibid.
13. *Kansas City Post*, 14 September 1907.
14. Goodman, *A Thrilling Record*, 27-28.

CHAPTER TWELVE—I Grew Sick of Killing Them

The title is borrowed from a remark attributed to Anderson by a *St Louis Daily Missouri Democrat* correspondent in reporting Anderson's torture of Benjamin Lewis at Glasgow on 21 October 1864.

1. *HBC*, 452. The county history is the main source for my general account of the battle at Singleton's farm. All dialogue and quotes not otherwise identified are taken from this source.
2. It's uncertain who led the small party that lured Johnston into the guerrilla trap. Watts said Clement did, McCorkle and Frank James said Pool, and the *HBC* said the small band was part of Thrailkill's command.
3. The *Columbia Missouri Herald*, 24 September 1897.
4. Goodman, *A Thrilling Record*, 33.
5. *OR*, vol. 41, pt. 1, 440.
6. *OR*, vol. 41, pt. 3, 489.
7. Goodman, *A Thrilling Record*, 38.

CHAPTER THIRTEEN—I Could Not Throw My Life Away
The title is borrowed from a remark attributed to Anderson by Edwards.

1. *St. Joseph Weekly Herald and Tribune*, 20 October 1864. See also Goodman, *A Thrilling Record*. I've relied mainly on these two sources for my account of the guerrillas' movements in the days following the Centralia massacre.

2. Goodman, *A Thrilling Record*, 44.

3. Ibid., 38.

4. Ibid., 44.

5. *OR*, vol. 41, pt. 3, 454.

6. Ibid., 455.

7. Ibid., 592.

8. Ibid.

9. *OR*, vol. 41, pt. 4, 354.

10. The correspondence of an officer at Warrenton (*OR*, vol. 41, pt. 3, 893) on 15 October 1864 says that the Danville raid occurred that same day, but a preponderance of later evidence indicates it happened the previous evening.

11. *The History of St. Charles, Montgomery, and Warren Counties*, 647-655, is the principal source for the sacking of Danville, including all quotes. See also the officer's correspondence cited in the previous note, Kemper's Civil War Reminiscences, and *OR*, vol. 41, pt. 1, 888.

12. *OR*, vol. 41, pt. 1, 632.

13. This dialogue and other events surrounding Anderson's visit to the Lewis home: *St. Louis Daily Missouri Democrat*, 12 November 1864. See also *Gallatin North Missourian*, 3 November 1864.

14. Lewis died in early 1866 from a carbuncle on his neck, but an obituary notice in the *Glasgow Times* (quoted in the 9 February 1866 *CMS*) at the time of his death gives no indication that his maltreatment at the hands of Anderson contributed to his demise.

15. HCC, 362.

16. *OR*, vol. 41, pt. 4, 727.

17. The date of Anderson's death is sometimes cited as October 26. Major Cox's own report (as given in *OR*, vol. 41, pt. 1, 442) is dated October 27 and indicates that the death occurred the previous day. However, a preponderance of other evidence suggests that the actual date of Anderson's death was the twenty-seventh. For instance, the October 30 *St. Joseph Herald and Tribune*, quotes the text of Cox's report and gives its date as October 28. In addition, several military correspondences shortly after Anderson's death cite October 27 as the date of the event.

18. Edwards, *Noted Guerrillas*, 326.

CHAPTER FOURTEEN—One Devil Less in the World
The title is taken from the 6 November 1864 *St. Louis Missouri Republican* in which the editor, upon viewing a photo of Anderson's body, reflects on the guerrilla's death.

1. *OR*, vol. 41, pt. 4, 354. A 31 October 1864 report by an unnamed

Federal officer reprinted in the 19 December 1986 *Richmond (Mo.) Daily News* also cites the flag inscription but correctly gives Anderson's middle initial as "T" rather than "L." Bill's full name, as it appeared on both the 1860 census and his marriage certificate, was William T. Anderson. (The "T" may have stood for Thomas. A Thomas Anderson, very likely Bill's grandfather, is listed in early Hopkins County, Kentucky, censuses in the same vicinity as William Thomasson and his father, Samuel Thomasson.)

    2. Rumor has it that on the evening after Anderson was killed, his head was cut off and the head placed on top of a telegraph pole as soldiers dragged the body through the streets of Richmond behind a horse to the hurrahs of an enthusiastic audience. Although the soldiers' dragging of the body seems credible, there appears to be no documentation for the more sensational variations of the legend.

    3. *St. Louis Daily Missouri Democrat,* 3 November 1864.
    4. *Liberty (Mo.) Tribune,* 11 November 1864.
    5. *St. Louis Daily Missouri Democrat,* 3 November 1864.
    6. Ibid.
    7. *CMS,* 2 September 1864.
    8. Ibid., 30 September 1864.
    9. *St. Louis Daily Missouri Democrat,* 29 September 1864.
    10. Ibid., 12 November 1864.
    11. *OR,* vol. 41, pt. 2, 690.
    12. Castel, *William Clarke Quantrill,* 179.

Bibliography

BOOKS, MANUSCRIPTS, PERIODICALS

Barth, Moses. Papers. Western Historical Manuscript Collection, University of Missouri at Columbia.

Barton, Fred. "Bill Anderson and Not Charlie Quantrell." Undated newspaper clipping in William Connelley Collection at Denver Public Library.

Barton, O. S. *Three Years with Quantrill: A True Story Told by His Scout John McCorkle.* 1914 (reprint). Norman: University of Oklahoma Press, 1992.

Britton, Wiley. *The Civil War on the Border* (2 vols.). New York: G.P. Putnam's Sons, 1899.

Brownlee, Richard. *Gray Ghosts of the Confederacy: Guerrilla Warfare in the West, 1861-1865.* Baton Rouge: Louisiana State University Press, 1958.

Castel, Albert. *A Frontier State at War: Kansas, 1861-65.* Ithaca (NY): Cornell University Press, 1958.

———. "Kansas Jayhawking Raids into Western Missouri in 1861." *Missouri Historical Review* 54 (October 1959): 1-11.

———. *William Clarke Quantrill: His Life and Times.* New York: Frederick Fell, Inc., 1962.

——— and Thomas Goodrich. *Bloody Bill Anderson: The Short Savage Life of a Civil War Guerrilla.* Mechanicsburg (PA): Stackpole Books, 1998.

"The Civil War in Missouri 1861-1865" Centennial Commission of Missouri, undated.

Clippings. Bill Anderson File. Missouri State Historical Society. Columbia, Mo., various dates.

Connelley, William E. *The Life of Preston B. Plumb.* Chicago: Browne & Howell Co., 1913.

———. Papers. Box 13. Kansas State Historical Society, Topeka.

———. *Quantrill and the Border Wars*, Cedar Rapids (IA): The Torch Press, 1910.
Cordley, Richard. *A History of Lawrence, Kansas*. Lawrence: Lawrence Journal Press, 1895.
Cutler, William G. *History of the State of Kansas*. 2 vols. Chicago: A. T. Andreas, 1883.
Cummins, Jim. *Jim Cummins' Book Written by Himself*. Denver: Reed Publishing Co., 1903.
Dix, Mrs. R. C. "Quantrill's Raid—an Eyewitness Account." *Westport Historical Quarterly*, vol. 1, no. 1 (May 1965): 8-11.
Doerschuk, Albert N. "Extracts from War-Time Letters, 1861-1864." *Missouri Historical Review* 23 (October 1928): 99-110.
Edwards, John N. *Noted Guerillas*. St. Louis: Bryan, Brand & Company, 1877.
Fellman, Michael. *Inside War*. New York: Oxford University Press, 1989.
Garwood, Darrell. *Crossroads of America: The Story of Kansas City*. New York: W. W. Norton Co. Inc., 1948.
Goodman, Thomas M., Sgt. *A Thrilling Record*. 1868 (Reprint). Maryville (MO): Rush Printing Co., 1960.
Goodrich, Thomas. *Black Flag: Guerrilla Warfare on the Western Border, 1861-1865*. Bloomington: Indiana University Press, 1995.
———. *Bloody Dawn*. Kent (OH): Kent State University Press, 1991.
Green, Charles R. *Early Days in Kansas*. Vols. 1 & 2. Olathe (KS): Charles R. Green, 1912.
Gregg, William H. *A Little Dab of History without Embelishment* [sic]. Unpublished Manuscript. Western Historical Manuscript Collection, University of Missouri, Columbia.
———. "The Lawrence Raid." Civil War Narratives. Kansas State Historical Society.
Hale, Donald R. *They Called Him Bloody Bill*. Clinton (MO): The Printery, 1975.
———. *We Rode with Quantrill*. Lee's Summit (MO): Donald R. Hale, 1982.
Harris, Charles F. "Catalyst for Terror: The Collapse of the Women's Prison in Kansas City." *Missouri Historical Review* 89 (April 1995): 290-306.
History of Boone County. St. Louis: Western Historical Co., 1882.
History of Carroll County. St. Louis: Missouri Historical Company, 1881.
History of Clay and Platte Counties, Missouri. St. Louis: National Historical Company, 1885.
History of Greene County, Missouri. (1883.) Clinton (MO): The Printery, 1969.
History of Howard and Chariton Counties, Missouri. St. Louis: National Historical Company, 1883.
History of Monroe and Shelby Counties, Missouri. St. Louis: National Historical Company, 1884.
History of Randolph and Macon Counties, Missouri. St. Louis: National Historical Company, 1884.
History of St. Charles, Montgomery, and Warren Counties, Missouri. St. Louis: National Historical Company, 1885.
Hubbard, David. "Reminiscences of the Yeager Raid, on the Santa Fe Trail, in 1863." *Transactions of the Kansas State Historical Society*, vol. 8 (1903-4): 168-171.

Kemper, Mary Lee. "Civil War Reminiscences at Danville Female Academy." *Missouri Historical Review* 62 (Spring 1968): 314-320.
Leslie, Edward E. *The Devil Knows How to Ride.* New York: Random House, 1996.
Levens, Henry C., and Nathaniel M. Drake. *A History of Cooper County, Missouri.* St. Louis: Perrin & Smith, 1876.
Marriage Records of Grayson County, Texas.
Marriage Records of Hopkins County, Kentucky.
McLarty, Vivian K., ed. "The Civil War Letters of Colonel Bazel Lazear," pt. 2, *Missouri Historical Review* 45 (July 1950): 387-401.
Monaghan, Jay. *Civil War on the Western Border, 1854-1865.* Boston: Little, Brown, 1955.
Morehouse, George Pierson. "Diamond Springs, 'The Diamond of the Plains.'" *Collections of the Kansas State Historical Society* 14 (1915-18): 794-804.
Pigg, Elmer L. "Bloody Bill, Noted Guerrilla of the Civil War." *The Trail Guide,* vol. 1, no. 4 (December 1956): 17-28.
Population Schedules of Sixth, Seventh, and Eighth Censuses of the United States. Washington, D.C., The National Archives and Records Service.
Rodemyre, Edgar T. *History of Centralia, Missouri.* Centralia: Press of the Fireside Guard, 1936.
Shea, John C., ed. *Reminiscences of Quantrell's Raid upon the City of Lawrence.* Kansas City (MO): Isaac P. Moore, 1897.
Shimeall, William Michael. *Arthur Inghram Baker: Frontier Kansan.* Emporia (KS): Emporia State University (master's thesis), 1978.
Switzler, William F. *History of Missouri.* 1877 (reprint). New York: Arno Press, 1975.
Thruston, Ethylene Ballard. "Captain Dick Yeager—Quantrill Man." *The Westport Historical Quarterly,* vol. 4 (June 1968): 3-4.
War of the Rebellion: A Compilation of Official Records of the Union and Confederate Armies. Washington, D.C.: Government Printing Office, 1880-1902.
Watts, Hamp B. *The Babe of the Company.* Fayette (MO): Democrat-Leader Press, 1913.
Younger, Cole. *The Story of Cole Younger by Himself,* 1903 (reprint). Springfield (MO): Oak Hills Publishing, 1996.

NEWSPAPERS

Boonville (Mo.) Weekly Monitor, 1864.
Brunswick (Mo.) Brunswicker, 1982.
Caldwell County Banner of Liberty, 1864.
Carrolton (Mo.) Democrat, 1864.
Columbia Missouri Herald, 1897.
Columbia Missouri Statesman, 1864.
Council Grove (Kans.) Press, 1860-1863.
Emporia (Kans.) News, 1859-1863.
Gallatin North Missourian, 1864.

Junction City Smoky Hill and Republican Union, 1862.
Kansas City (Mo.) Daily Journal of Commerce, 1862-1864.
Kansas City (Mo.) Journal, 1888.
Kansas City (Mo.) Post, 1907, 1915.
Kansas City (Mo.) Star, 1913, 1929. 1957, 1959.
Kansas City (Mo.) Weekly Journal of Commerce, 1864.
Kansas Cosmos, 1886.
Kansas Press, 1859-1860.
Leavenworth Daily Conservative, 1863.
Lexington (Mo.) Weekly Union, 1863.
Liberty (Mo.) Tribune, 1864.
Macon (Mo.) Gazette, 1864.
Moberly (Mo.) Message, 1934.
Palymyra Missouri Whig and General Advertiser, 1840-1841.
Richmond (Mo.) Daily News, 1986.
St. Joseph Herald and Tribune, 1864.
St. Joseph Morning Herald, 1864.
St. Joseph Weekly Herald and Tribune, 1864.
St. Louis Daily Missouri Democrat, 1864.
St. Louis Missouri Republican, 1864
St. Louis Republic, 1899.
White Cloud Kansas Chief, 1862.
Wyandotte (Kans.) Commercial Gazette, 1863.

Index

Agnes City, Kansas, 6, 12, 15, 16
Albany, battle, 134-135
Albany, Missouri, 134
alcohol. *See* whiskey
Allen, Missouri, 83
Anderson, Ellis, 1, 10, 11
Anderson, James, 1, 11, 17, 18, 19, 88, 139, 141
Anderson, Josephine, 1, 29, 30, 31
Anderson, Martha "Mattie," 30, 31-32
Anderson, Martha, 1, 4, 11,
Anderson, Martha Jane "Janie," 1, 31
Anderson, Mary "Molly," 12, 13, 15, 29, 30, 32
Anderson, Mary Ellen, 1
Anderson, Thomas, 2
Anderson, W. L., 136
Anderson, William C., 1, 2, 3, 4, 6, 10-11, 12, 15, 81
Anderson, William "Bloody Bill"
  ancestry of, 2
  and Baxter Springs massacre, 56
  birth of, 1
  as captain, 63
  death of, xi, 96-97, 134, 135, 136, 137, 138, 139, 140
  description of, 11, 22, 124
  early gang of, 11-12, 14-15, 18-20, 21, 22, 60
  employment of, 6, 10, 11
  and guerilla warfare, 10, 16, 22, 34, 45, 70, 71
  horse of, 15, 133
  and horse stealing, 11, 12, 14
  and Lawrence Massacre, 35, 37, 44, 48
  as lieutenant, 25, 60
  letters by, 70, 72-73, 75, 84
  and litigation, 15-16
  loyalty of, 14-15, 16, 20, 28, 30, 34, 45, 71, 136
  marriage of, 57, 59
  opinions of, xi, xii, 1, 3, 6, 11, 12, 16, 22, 83, 94-95, 102, 135, 141
  peacemaking of, 15, 19, 40, 44, 80, 81, 86, 106
  and Quantrill, William, xi, 17, 22, 56, 59, 60, 61, 62, 63, 83, 94, 101, 102, 138, 141
  weaponry of, 80, 136, 138
  and whiskey, 125, 131-132
  youth of, 1, 3, 4, 5, 6, 8, 12, 15

Anthony, Daniel, 9
Anthony, Susan B., 9
arson. *See* vandalism
Atchison, Kansas, 4
Aubrey, Kansas, 9, 17, 39, 68
Austin, Henry, 3, 81
Austin, Tad, 3, 79-80, 81

Babe of the Company, The, 99
Bailey, L. D., 5
Baker, A. I., 6, 12-13, 14, 15, 16, 18
Baker, James, 2
Baker, Mahala, 2
Baker, ———, 92
Banks, Alexander, 42
Bates County, Missouri, 29, 52
Baum, Solomon, 76-77
Baxter Springs, Kansas, 53-58
Baxter Springs, massacre, 53-56, 58
Bell Air, Missouri, 65
Bell, Thomas, 75
Benton, ———, 104
Berry, ———, 131, 132
Bigknife (Shawnee), 28
Bingham, George Caleb, 31, 33
Bingham, Mrs. George Caleb, 31
Blackwater River, Missouri, 37, 53
Bledsoe, Jim, 46, 48, 57
Bluff Creek, Kansas, 5, 8, 11, 12
Blunt, Andy, 52, 73
Blunt, James G., 29, 55, 56
Bonham, Texas, 61
Bookout, Wright, 27
Boone County, Missouri, 106-116
Boone County raid, 106-116. *See also* Centralia, massacre
Breckinridge County, Kansas, 6, 12, 13, 16. *See also* Lyon County
Breitenbaugh, Sam, 26
Briggs, ———, 83
Brooklyn, Kansas, 50
Brown, Egbert B., 64, 68, 69, 72, 75
Brown, John, 4, 9
Brown, John, Jr., 9
Brownfield, Mr., 66
Brownlee, Richard, 34, 99

Bryson, G. W., 105, 117
Buffington (steamer), 99
Burris, ———, 72, 73
Butts, Major, 59, 60, 61

Calvert, Captain, 77
Calvert, Nancy, 89
Carroll County "the Gourd," Missouri, 75, 76, 78, 93, 94, 133
Carroll County History, 96
Carroll County, raid, 75-78, 93-94
Carrollton Democrat, 93
Cass County, Missouri, 29, 52
Central District of Missouri, 67
Centralia, battle, 117-122
Centralia, massacre, xi, 106-116, 122, 126, 131, 133, 141
Centralia, Missouri, 106, 116, 122, 127
Chapman, ———, 96
Chariton County, Missouri, 78
Childs, Colonel, 26
City Hotel, 46
Civil War, causes of, 3-7, 9-10
Clark, James, 108, 109, 114
Clarke, Kate, 25, 78, 101, 102. *See also* King, Kate
Clement, Arch "Little Archie," 48, 66-67, 76, 84, 85, 86, 96, 109, 111, 112, 113, 121, 130, 133, 139
Clement, ———, 67
Cleveland, Marshall, 9
Coleman, Charles F., 27, 28, 50
Collamore, George W., 44
Colley, Patten, 94
Collier, J. J., 106
Columbia Missouri Statesman, 78, 82, 83, 84, 86, 88, 99, 141
Comanches, 59
Company M, 72
Connelley, William E., 48, 141
Contributive Tax, 100-101
Cooper County, Missouri, 65
Cooper, Douglas, 58
Cooper, Joseph, 64
Council Bluffs, Iowa, 10

Council Grove, Kansas, 5, 11, 17
Council Grove Press, 12
Cox, Samuel P. "Cob," 134, 138, 139
Craig, James, 134, 138
Crawford, Riley, 56, 57
Cummins, Jim, 82-83
Curtis, Samuel R., 68

Damon, George, 80-81
Daniels, John, 84
Danville, massacre, 129-130
Darr, William, 88, 89
decapitation. *See* mutilation
Delawares, 51-52
Democratic Congressional Convention, 107
DeMoyne, George, 11-12
Denny, A. F., 87-88, 104
Denny, Mr., 87-88
Department of Kansas, 68
Department of Missouri, 68
District of Central Missouri, 64
District of Kansas, 29, 55
District of North Missouri, 86
District of the Border, 29, 31
District of the Frontier, 29, 55
Dix, Getta, 43
Dix, Ralph, 42-43
Douglass, J. B., 86, 98, 123
Dugan, Isaac W., 89-90

Edwards, John N., 35, 36, 48, 135, 141
Eighth Military District, 86
Eisenhour, ———, 133
Emory, ———, 100
Emporia News, 11, 14, 15, 20
Ervin, ———, 75
Erwin, ———, 69
Etter, ———, 133
Ewing, Thomas, 26, 29, 30, 31, 32, 36, 49, 52

Fayette, Missouri, 102-104
Fickle, Anna, 73
First Iowa Cavalry, 108

Fisk, Clinton B., 86, 94, 104, 126, 127, 141
Forson, Samuel, 95
Fort Blair, Missouri, 53, 55-56
Fort Scott, Missouri, 13, 55
Fort Sumter, South Carolina, 7
Fourteenth Kansas Cavalry, 55
Fourth Missouri Cavalry, 98
Fox, ———, 96
Fredericksburg, Missouri, 94
Free-State Party, 6

Glasgow, massacre, 131-133, 141
Glasgow, Missouri, 131, 133
Goodman, Thomas, 112, 113, 116, 121, 125, 126, 127
Graham, William, 92
Grand Avenue building, 31-34, 35. *See also* McGee's Addition
Grandstaff, Mollie, 30
Gray, Joe, 28
Gray, Mrs. (nee Mundy, Lucinda), 30
Gregg, William, 17, 46, 53, 55, 58
Griffin, Lee, 12, 13, 14, 15, 18, 21
Griffith, Hiram, 76
Grimes, John, 96
Griswold, Jerome, 44
Grovenor, Gurdon, 44, 45
Grovenor, Mrs., 44, 45
guerrilla warfare, causes of, xi, 3-7, 35

Hale, Donald R., 139
Hamlet, Jesse, 75
Harris, ———, 20
Hartgrove, ———, 76
Harvey, Captain, 27
Hays, John, 92
Henderson, ———, 92
Henry, ———, 18
Henry County, Missouri 29
Henry, John, 77
Hesper, Kansas, 40
Higbee, ———, 65
High Hill, Missouri, 130
Hinton, ———, 73

History of Boone County, 107, 110, 113, 117, 120
History of Carroll County, 78, 88, 89, 93, 133
History of Monroe and Shelby County, 87
History of St. Charles, Montgomery and Warren Counties, The, 129
Holt, John D., 39, 48, 53
Holtzclaw, Clifton, 97, 98
Hopkins County, Kentucky, 1
Howard County, Missouri, 78, 98
Hoyt, George, 9
Hume, ———, 78
Huntsville, Missouri, 3, 78, 79-81, 84-86, 88
Hurricane Township, Missouri, 89-90
Hutchinson, James, 65
Hutchinson, Mrs. James, 65

Illinois Cavalry, 84
Independent Order of Odd Fellows, 3

Jackson County, Missouri, 7, 9, 10, 21, 22, 29, 52, 64
Jacoby, William, 19
James, Frank, 35, 48, 82, 94, 96, 104, 120
James, Jesse, 35, 82, 94, 96-97, 120
Jennison, Charles "Doc," 7, 9, 45
Jewell, L. R., 13
Johnson County, Missouri, 29, 53, 66
Johnson, Missouri, 28, 72
Johnston, A. V. E., 105, 117, 118, 119, 120, 122, 134

Kansas Brigade, 9
Kansas City and Council Grove Stage Company, 19
Kansas City and Santa Fe Mail Company, 19
Kansas City Daily Journal of Commerce, 24, 31, 33, 68
Kansas City, Kansas, 7
Kansas First Cavalry, 67, 72
Kansas-Nebraska Act, 3-4
Kansas Press, 11

Kaws, 10
Kelly, ———, 95-96
King, Kate, 25. *See also* Clarke, Kate
Kingsville, Missouri, 72
Kirkby, Jack, 109
Kirker, John, 90
Knapp, Ebenezer, 83, 84
Koger, John, 119

Lafayette County, Missouri, 25-26, 29, 73
Lane, Jim, 9, 35, 44, 50, 133
Latham, ———, 92
Lawrence, Amos, 35
Lawrence, Kansas, xi, 4, 36, 48
Lawrence, massacre, xi, 35-39, 41-48, 51, 52, 58, 90
Lazear, Bazel F., 52
Leavenworth, Kansas, 4
Lee, Dudley, 46, 139
Leland, Cyrus, Jr., 49
Leonard, Leverett, 65
Leonard, Nathaniel, 65
Leonard, Reeves, 98, 99, 101, 102
Lewis, Benjamin W., 131, 132-133, 141
Lewis, Mrs., 131, 132
Lexington, Missouri, 27, 71, 72, 73, 75
Lexington Union, 25
Lexington Weekly Union, 21
Liberty Tribune, 94
Live Oak (steamer), 69
looting. *See* vandalism
Long, Peyton, 48, 96, 110
Lyon County, Kansas, 13. *See also* Breckinridge County, Kansas
Lyon, Nathaniel, 13
Lyons, Cyrus, 77, 78

Marney, ———, 83
Mars (steamer), 100
Martin, J., 62, 63
Matthews, Edwin, 77
Matthews, Thomas, 92
Maupin, James, 95

Maupin, John, 90
Mayo, William H., 65-66
McCorkle, Jabez, 32
McCorkle, John, 32, 34, 35
McCorkle, Nannie Harris, 32
McCulloch, Henry, 58-59, 60, 61-62, 63
McFerran, Colonel, 26, 70, 71-72, 73
McGee's Addition, 33. *See also* Grand Avenue building
McMurtry, Lee, 100
Milton, Missouri, 126
Mineral Creek, Texas, 58
Missouri Compromise, 3-4
Missouri State Guard, 13
Mitchell, Caroline, 89, 90
Mitchell, Mary, 89
Mitchell, Stephen, 92
Mitchell, Susan, 89
Montgomery County, Missouri, 129
Montgomery, James, 9
Moonlight, Thomas, 68
Moore, ———, 129
Morgan, ———, 60
Mundy, Lucinda. *See* Gray, Mrs.
Mundy, Martha, 30
Mundy, Sue, 30
mutilation, 4-5, 90, 94, 122
    decapitation, 90, 91, 100, 102, 121, 133, 136
    scalping, 46, 52, 67, 84, 90, 91, 95, 98, 99, 101, 102, 104, 111, 112, 122, 128

Nance, Mrs. John, 92
Neet, ———, 76
Neill, Henry, 21
New England Emigrant Aid Company, 35
New Florence, Missouri, 130
Nichols, John, 84
Ninth Cavalry, 27, 82, 101, 102

O'Dell, Benjamin, 19, 39-40
O'Dell, O. F., 15, 19
Ogden, William, 26

Oliphant, ———, 93
Omaha (steamer), 97
Osceola, Missouri, 9

Palmyra, Missouri, 1
Parke, Joseph, 98-99
Parker, Ben, 26
Parker, Charlie, 3, 11
Parman, Joseph, 67, 71
Partisan Ranger Act, 24
Payne, Stephen J., 28
Perdee, Captain, 37
Perkins, Caleb, 105
Peters, Valentine, 112-113
Pike, J. A., 39, 49
Pinson, Josiah, 13
Pinson, Richard, 13
Plumb, Preston B., 32, 49, 50
Pond, James B., 53, 55
Pool, Dave, 26, 55, 68, 119, 121, 134, 139
Post Boy (steamer), 69
Pottawatomie Creek, Kansas, 4
Pratt, Dick, 11
Price, Sterling, 7, 9, 13, 58, 59, 63, 105, 128, 136

Quantrill, William
    and Anderson, William "Bloody Bill," xi, 17, 22, 56, 59, 60, 61, 62, 63, 83, 941, 101, 102, 138, 141
    and Baxter Springs massacre, 53, 55, 56, 58
    betrayal of, 58, 61-62, 63, 102, 103
    Confederate rank of, 24, 60
    direct orders of, 41, 42, 52, 53, 58, 59, 60
    and guerrilla warfare, 9, 35
    horse of, 63
    and Lawrence massacre, 35-39, 49-50, 51, 58
    leadership of, xi, 9, 10, 17, 24-25, 35-36, 38, 39, 51, 53, 58, 59-60, 78, 94, 102, 103, 139
    and litigation, 61-62, 63

168   BLOODY BILL ANDERSON

photo of, 23
and whiskey, 56, 58

railroad depots, 83, 87, 106-114, 128, 130, 131. *See also* Centralia, massacre; vandalism
Rains, James S., 13, 134
Randolph County, Missouri, 1, 87-88, 126
Randolph Lodge 23, 3
Ratliff, John W., 13
Ray County, Missouri, 94
Red Legs, 7, 9, 27, 42-43
Reed, William, 18, 21, 22
Rice, ———, 19-20
Richmond, Missouri, 136, 138
Richmond, Virginia, 24
Rocheport, Missouri, 98, 99, 127
Rock Creek, Kansas, 13, 15
Rollins, James S., 107
Rosecrans, William S., 68, 75, 126
Rote, Jacob, 40, 46
Rothrock, Mr., 49
Rothrock, Mrs., 49
Rucker, ———, 100
Ruggles, Robert M., 16
Russell, ———, 92-93

Santa Fe Trail, 3, 5, 8, 12
Saunders, ———, 87
Sauvinet, Mr., 79, 80-81
Sauvinet, Mrs., 81
Saviers, ———, 27
scalping. *See* mutilation
Second Colored Regiment, 41
Segur, Annis, 13, 16
Segur, George, 18
Segur, Ira, 13-14
Seventeenth Illinois Cavalry, 83, 97
Seventh Kansas Cavalry, 7
Seventh Military District of Missouri, 138
Sewell, Eli, 6, 10, 11, 14, 16
Shanklin, Colonel, 94
Shawnees, 128
Shelbina, Missouri, 87

Shelby, General, 69, 131, 141
Sherman, Texas, 59, 60, 141
Simons, ———, 130
Singleton, M. G., 105
Sixth Kansas Cavalry, 13, 27
Skaggs, Larkin, 41, 42, 46, 48
slavery, 3-6
Smith, Bush, 57, 59, 60
Smith, Frank, 102
Sneed, A. F., 106, 117, 118, 122
Sneed, Thomas, 114, 118
Sni Hills, Missouri, 9, 25, 67, 78
Snider, Henry, 78
Snyder, S. S., 41
St. Clair County, Missouri, 29
St. Joseph Morning Herald, 94
St. Louis Daily Missouri Democrat, 132, 141
Stafford, John E., 118, 121
steamers, 68-69, 82, 97, 99-100. *See also* vandalism
Stewart, John, 24
Stone, Joseph, 40
Stone, Lydia, 46
Stone, Nathan, 46
Strieby, C. H., 13
Sturgeon, Missouri, 82, 86
Subdistrict of North Texas, 58

Taylor, Fletch, 60, 61, 88, 87, 94
Thacher, T. Dwight, 24
Theis, Adam, 118, 121
Third Wisconsin Cavalry, 55
Thirty-ninth Missouri Infantry Volunteers, 105, 117
Thomasson, Mahala, 1
Thomasson, Martha J., 2
Thomasson, Samuel, 2
Thomasson, William, 1, 2
Thornton, ———, 94
Thorpe, S. M., 44
Thrailkill, John, 94, 101, 102, 119, 120
Three Years with Quantrill, 35
Todd, George, 9, 25, 36, 40, 42, 43, 45, 48, 50, 56, 58, 60, 62, 63, 78,

94, 101, 104, 117, 118, 119, 120, 125, 139
Trask, Josiah F., 44
Tucker, John, 65
Turner, Mrs., 101

Union Hotel, 31
Union army, military strategies of, 29-30, 31, 32, 33, 36, 49-50, 55, 68, 78, 86, 94-95, 97, 117-118, 126-127, 134

vandalism, 5, 7, 9
    arson, 5, 7, 9, 18, 19, 24, 28, 42, 44, 45, 46, 49, 50, 65, 92, 95, 113, 114, 129, 130
    looting, 7, 18, 19, 24, 27, 28, 56, 59 ,65, 66, 76, 77, 78, 79, 80, 81, 82, 83, 87, 92, 93, 94, 95, 100-101, 106-107, 110, 111, 114, 130, 129
    and railroad depots, 83, 87, 106-114, 128, 130, 131
    and steamers, 68-69, 82, 97, 99-100
Vanzant, Daniel, 95
Vernon County, Missouri, 29, 52
Viley, John, 104

War Eagle (steamer), 82
Warren, James, 95

Warrensburg, Missouri, 73
Waterman, Thomas, 99
Watts, Hamp, 99, 100, 103, 104
Waugh, James H., 107, 108
weaponry, types of, 39, 53, 55, 71, 80, 89, 107, 109, 112, 117, 118, 119, 122, 123, 128, 134, 138
Wellington, Missouri, 68-69
West Wind (steamer), 68
whiskey, 11, 42, 56, 58, 107, 116, 125
White Turkey (Delaware), 51-52
Willis, Hannah, 2
Wilson, Mrs., 32
Withington, C. H., 16, 19
women, 41, 73, 75, 90-91, 130
    and children, 41, 73, 90, 129-130, 132, 133
    and the Grand Avenue Building, 31-34
    roles of, 29, 30, 33, 39, 73, 89, 100
Woolfork, ———, 66
Wyandotte County, Kansas, 27-28
Wyandotte County, massacre, 27-28
Wyatt, Cave, 111

Yeager, Dick, 22, 24, 66, 67
Yellowstone (steamer), 99-100
Younger, Cole, xi, 9, 22, 32, 34, 58, 139
Younger, Mr., 34-35

About the Author

Larry Wood is a retired public school teacher who now concentrates full time on writing. He has sold articles and stories to numerous regional and national publications, including *America's Civil War, Blue and Gray* magazine, *Kansas!, Missouri Life, The Ozarks Mountaineer, Reader's Digest, True West,* and *Wild West.*

Wood is a lifelong Missouri resident, and the conflict along the Missouri-Kansas border during the Civil War has long been of special interest to him. He has published several articles on the subject, including a brief biography of Bill Anderson in the Summer 2000 issue of *Gateway Heritage,* a publication of the Missouri Historical Society. He is also the author of *The Civil War on the Lower Kansas-Missouri Border,* published by Hickory Press.

Wood is a member of the Western Writers of America, and for the past eight years he has been an instructor for the Long Ridge Writers Group correspondence school of Long Ridge, Connecticut. He and his wife have one adult son, and they live in Joplin, Missouri.

www.ingramcontent.com/pod-product-compliance
Lightning Source LLC
Chambersburg PA
CBHW070552160426
43199CB00014B/2470